The Norman Conquest: A Very Short Introduction

VERY SHORT INTRODUCTIONS are for anyone wanting a stimulating and accessible way into a new subject. They are written by experts, and have been translated into more than 45 different languages.

The series began in 1995, and now covers a wide variety of topics in every discipline. The VSI library now contains over 500 volumes—a Very Short Introduction to everything from Psychology and Philosophy of Science to American History and Relativity—and continues to grow in every subject area.

Titles in the series include the following:

George Garnett

THE NORMAN CONQUEST

A Very Short Introduction

OXFORD
UNIVERSITY PRESS

OXFORD

UNIVERSITY PRESS

Great Clarendon Street, Oxford ox2 6DP

Oxford University Press is a department of the University of Oxford.
It furthers the University's objective of excellence in research, scholarship,
and education by publishing worldwide in

Oxford New York

Auckland Cape Town Dar es Salaam Hong Kong Karachi
Kuala Lumpur Madrid Melbourne Mexico City Nairobi
New Delhi Shanghai Taipei Toronto

With offices in

Argentina Austria Brazil Chile Czech Republic France Greece
Guatemala Hungary Italy Japan Poland Portugal Singapore
South Korea Switzerland Thailand Turkey Ukraine Vietnam

Oxford is a registered trade mark of Oxford University Press
in the UK and in certain other countries

Published in the United States
by Oxford University Press Inc., New York

British Library Cataloguing in Publication Data

Data available

Library of Congress Cataloging in Publication Data

Data available

Typeset by SPI Publisher Services, Pondicherry, India
Printed in Great Britain by
Ashford Colour Press Ltd, Gosport, Hampshire

ISBN 978-0-19-2801616

Impression: 12

For Elinor, Edmund, and Gregory

Contents

Preface

This little book recasts an interpretation of the Norman Conquest which I have developed in previous publications. The brevity of the *Very Short Introduction* format has encouraged a more trenchant statement of that interpretation, which may or may not be welcome. But the need to recast has led me to see many points which had previously eluded me, and to explore in some detail a subject which, on a scholarly level, was new to me—Romanesque architecture in England. Architecture is the most visible and therefore obvious remnant of the Conquest, and it merits detailed consideration in a work intended to introduce the non-specialist to the subject. The book is therefore more than a précis of some of my published views. Writing it has been a pleasure.

Part of that pleasure has arisen from the fact that the format of the series prohibits footnotes. A drawback of this refreshing feature is that I have not been able to express my debts to those whose published work I have drawn on, other than by hints dropped in the References section at the end of the book. I hope that they will make allowances.

Many of those who have taken the Norman Conquest Special Subject in Oxford in recent years will recognize points which have suddenly become clear in the heat of tutorial discussion. I hope that they will not regard as inadequate this general acknowledgement of the stimulation they have provided in our collective exploration of the evidence.

I should like to thank those who have read the whole book in draft, several of them several times: John Blair, Lizzy Emerson, John Hudson, George Molyneaux, and Helen Pike. They have shown that it is possible to raise an eyebrow in a marginal comment, even (or perhaps especially) when it is written in purple ink. I have sometimes taken notice.

My colleagues at St Hugh's College and Lady Margaret Hall, and in the wider Faculty of Modern History, have been supportive in all sorts of ways. Debbie Quare, the librarian at St Hugh's, remains a brick.

My children have rightly pointed out to me that it is more than time that they had a book dedicated to them. So here it is, belatedly, but as promised.

St Hugh's College, Oxford
14 October 2008

List of illustrations

List of illustrations

I come to write of a time, wherein the State of *England* received an alteration of Lawes, Customes, Fashion, manner of living, Language, writing, with new formes of Fights, Fortifications, Buildings, and generally an innovation in most things, but religion: So that from this mutation, which was the greatest it ever had, we are to begin with a new account of an *England*, more in dominion abroad, more in State and ability at home, and of more honour and name in the world, than heretofore: which by being thus undone was made as it were, in the Fate thereof to get more by losing, than otherwise.

Samuel Daniel, *The Collection of the History of England* (1618).

Introduction

'Regime change' is a current, inelegant euphemism for the removal and replacement of a foreign government by force. It is a euphemism because it dodges two questions: who is effecting the change, and how? That the answers to these questions are nevertheless often simple and obvious serves to underline the Orwellian character of the euphemism. Of course, it also fails to indicate why an existing regime should be overthrown by foreign arms. The answer to this question is, by contrast, usually not self-evident. Partly for this reason, it is not veiled in a euphemism, but tackled head on. The ground for the recent, defining example of regime change in Iraq was prepared by elaborate efforts to justify such violent external intervention. The legitimacy of conquest was widely assumed to depend on demonstrating the illegitimacy, on a number of counts, of the regime which was to be changed. The change must be shown to be not only urgently necessary, but also right.

This book is concerned with regime change, 11th-century style. One of the characteristics which the Norman Conquest of England shares with 21st-century regime change is overwhelming violence. For reasons which will become clear, Duke William of Normandy chanced his arm with a large invasion force, amassed from all over western Francia, at the end of September 1066, in order to contest Harold II's recent accession as king of England. Four days before the Norman landings at Pevensey, King Harold had repulsed another, Norwegian-backed, invasion in the North, at the battle of Stamford Bridge. The victorious but insecure king had then rushed south to deal with the Norman incursion into Sussex. The accession of Harold, who was not of the English royal line, seems to have signalled an open season as far as claims to the English throne were concerned. Like Stamford Bridge, the battle of Hastings, fought on 14 October 1066, was an object lesson in why, in most circumstances, mass pitched battles tended to be avoided during this period. Defeat was likely to prove definitive, as it did in both these cases.

The sources for the battle of Hastings are much fuller than those for Stamford Bridge; indeed, they are much fuller than for most battles in the medieval period. But as is so often the case with the Norman Conquest as a whole, their comparative richness turns out to be a source of confusion rather than of clarity. The most detailed, nearly contemporary written account, by one of the duke's chaplains, William of Poitiers, c. 1077, self-consciously owes a great deal to Julius Caesar's descriptions of his campaigns, including his invasions of Britain, and to Vegetius' ancient manual on warfare. It was against antique standards that Duke William's military achievement would and should be judged. William of Poitiers even goes to the lengths of avoiding medieval Latin terminology, in his desire to write in the unalloyed language of classical Rome. But the Roman influence on him is not confined to linguistic purity, or baroque ornamentation. It is almost impossible to judge how far his account of the whole military campaign, including the battle, is distorted by the antique lenses he so ostentatiously deploys—all the more so because a slightly earlier, much more terse Norman account of these events, by William of Jumièges (c. 1071), shares almost no common ground with his. William of Jumièges is grittily matter-of-fact in style, and very few of his facts from the battle and subsequent campaign are repeated by William of Poitiers. Indeed, William of Poitiers' classical pretensions were not confined to aping matter-of-fact Roman authors like Caesar; by drawing on Virgil, Statius, and Lucan, and deriving stories from Homer and

Xenophon, he was already, a decade after the event, recasting the campaign of 1066 as an heroic triumph in the mould of antique epic. The Conqueror was not just compared to the first Roman conqueror of Britain; he was Achilles or Agamemnon or Aeneas *redivivus*. 'The authors of the *Thebaid* or the *Aeneid*, who in their books sing of great events, and by the law of poetry render them greater, could make an equally great and more worthy work by singing truthfully of the acts of this man.'

Whoever designed the Bayeux Tapestry, which also attempts to tell the whole story of the Conquest, clearly knew William of Poitiers' account—or the source or sources on which William based his account—well. These two related documents provide much the most detailed contemporary narratives of the battle: it takes up more than a quarter of what survives of the Tapestry. Many of the Tapestry's images are still more familiar than episodes related by William of Poitiers, but again, the harder we look at them, the less convincing they seem. Familiarity tends to breed an unreflective acceptance, which can be deceptive.

The Tapestry's narrative is, for obvious reasons, less detailed than a written account; and even when detailed, it does not always precisely corroborate William of Poitiers. For instance, William describes how the duke, realizing that he had lost contact with his fleet, held a banquet in mid-Channel in order to calm his jittery crew—an episode probably inspired by Aeneas doing something similar when shipwrecked on the African coast. The Tapestry portrays the banquet as having taken place on land, as Aeneas' had, and records that Odo, bishop of Bayeux, the duke's half-brother, blessed the food and wine. The designer's point here was not to draw a parallel between the duke and Aeneas, but to emphasize the central role of Odo, for whom the Tapestry seems to have been made. The echo was scriptural—of the Last Supper—not classical. That the Tapestry was commissioned by a very important participant in the Conquest, who is depicted as having played a key part in the battle, and that it is now thought

3

to have been embroidered by English needlewomen in the 1070s, does not mean that its narrative should be approached with any less circumspection than William of Poitiers'. This is also true of its depiction of material objects, including military equipment. In some respects, this too can be shown to be so stylized as to be deceptive: for instance, the Norman cavalry could not have worn chain-mail trousers, because doing so would have made it impossible to ride a horse.

The Tapestry's portrayal of the battle itself lacks some of the key episodes in William of Poitiers' account. Central to the latter was the duke's use of the tactic of feigned flight to break the English defences on the crest of the hill at the place which would become known as Battle. This was a tactic outlined by Vegetius, and it is impossible to be certain that the French forces adopted it in the battle, just as it is impossible to know whether William is accurate in recording that they were arrayed in three ranks—of archers, heavy infantry, and cavalry—just as Caesar says he deployed his troops. Neither the feigned flight nor the deployment in three ranks appear in the Tapestry. Although it depicts the Old English defensive shield wall also mentioned by William of Poitiers, otherwise it pays little attention to infantry and archers. The designer was overwhelmingly concerned with chivalry, in the literal sense of the word, with the deaths of Harold's brothers and of the king himself, and with the eventual rout of the English forces. He was so because this was what his audience wanted to see. The fullest accounts of the battle are therefore to a considerable degree works of art, as is the slightly later claim that the Norman forces advanced into battle reciting a medieval heroic poem, the Song of Roland.

All that is clear about the battle of Hastings is that it was decisive for the Norman attempt to contest Harold II's accession as king. This proved to be the case despite a brief series of desperate, last-ditch attempts on the part of the English to resist what the outcome of the battle had rendered almost inevitable. None of this is portrayed in the Tapestry, which breaks off at the end of the battle, possibly because it was never completed, or more likely because the final section has been lost. Duke William first moved east to Dover and Canterbury, and then circled London to the south and west, crossing the Thames at Wallingford. Eventually the remnants of the English establishment submitted to him at Berkhamsted in Hertfordshire. He was then ready to take London itself. These events were so swift and decisive that, according to William of Poitiers, the duke was able to relax and to go hunting and hawking. (He is depicted out hawking in Normandy in the Tapestry.) The wake of destruction left by Duke William's army in the campaign which followed Hastings can still be traced in the depleted land values recorded in the survey known as Domesday Book, compiled twenty years later.

The bloody events of 1066, culminating in William's coronation as king on Christmas Day (with which the original Tapestry probably concluded), were, however, only the start of the process of subjugation. In 1068, King Harold's sons, who had fled into exile, backed a rising based on Exeter; but the city prudently capitulated to William after a brief siege, apparently on terms similar to those offered to London, Winchester, and York. The rising fizzled out. A rebellion in the North in 1069, with the aim of restoring the Old English royal house, provoked a scorched earth response from King William, the effects of which are also manifest in Domesday Book. The chronicle accounts corroborate this statistical evidence: William's harrying of the North constituted 'shock and awe' even without the use of munitions.

Ruthless violence on this scale was necessary to enforce change of a magnitude and at a speed unparalleled in English history. Many of those important Englishmen who did not die fighting in the pitched battles of 1066 and the subsequent ineffectual attempts at resistance, or who did not flee into exile, quickly found themselves in pitifully diminished circumstances. Such a survivor might, for instance, be permitted to hold some of the land which had formerly been his from the Norman to whom the new king had given it. In that way he could secure protection of a sort in a very uncertain world, and salvage something from the wreckage. Or he might cut his losses by acting as steward for his replacement, becoming a hired retainer on the estate which had once been his. As the lugubrious author of one manuscript of the *Anglo-Saxon Chronicle* put it, at the conclusion of his entry for 1066, 'always after that it grew much worse'. This regime change amounted to a lot more than a change in regime.

The other characteristic which the Conquest shares with modern regime change is the heavy emphasis on justification. Many of the reasons why the Norman victors were so concerned to justify their actions are, unsurprisingly, quite different, but the concern is a common one, regardless of the intervening millennium. There are, however, two important distinctions, the second following from the first.

First, although the Norman Conquest resulted in the swiftest, most brutal, and most far-reaching transformation in English history, it was not justified as a change of regime. On the contrary, the Normans claimed that they were the old regime continued. The existing kingdom of England was not even under new management, for, it was argued, Duke William was the sole legitimate heir to the English throne. King Edward the Confessor, regarded by the Normans as the last Old English king, had nominated William as such. There had been no change at all. Even the fact that William had conquered England by defeating Edward's immediate successor, King Harold II, the former earl of Wessex—deemed a usurper by the Normans—was progressively excised from the historical record.

Second, the elaboration of this fiction of continuity rapidly transformed England into something which Englishmen prior to 1066 would have found it increasingly difficult to recognize. The exceptionally precocious apparatus of royal government, which seems to have been one of the distinctive characteristics of the English kingdom since its creation in the early 10th century, was carefully preserved. Indeed, it was only by means of it that much of the transformation was accomplished. In the fundamental case of landholding, for instance, this was true not only of the replacement of individual landholders, but of the very system of tenure. These changes would have been impossible without the Old English institutions of the shire and its constituent hundreds, each of which was composed of (usually) one hundred hides, a hide being the standard unit of fiscal land assessment. Each shire and each constituent hundred had its own public court, the *fora* in which grants of land were publicized. The changes would also have been impossible without the apparatus of royal bureaucracy: chiefly the royal writing office, through which the king issued his instructions, primarily in terse Old English documents known as writs. It was in this way that he communicated with the sheriff, the royal administrator in each shire who usually presided (alongside the bishop) in the shire court.

Yet the form which the transformation took was determined not by the governmental system through which it was imposed on conquered England, but by the fiction of continuity, grounded in the justification of William the Conqueror's position of king. Thereby this fiction insinuated itself into the very structure of the kingdom, rapidly transforming it into something quite different from King Edward the Confessor's England, the maintenance of which nevertheless rapidly became the Conqueror's mantra. Like most mantras, its literal meaning was the opposite of its true one. The more continuity was bruited, the less continuity there was.

A tenurial transformation of this magnitude, effected in the name of maintaining the *status quo*, necessarily entailed other massive changes. Law is perhaps the most obvious case, for, as J. C. Holt argues, if 'Legitimacy became beautiful in [the Normans'] sight', then it must be established by law. Because this was true of the king's claim to the kingdom, it was also true of all those who, as a result of his successful assertion of that claim, were deemed to hold their lands of him. We shall see that very soon after the Conquest, everyone acknowledged that he did so, either immediately of the king, or intermediately, that is to say, through a lord who held directly of the king. It can be shown that this had simply not been the case in Edward the Confessor's England. But law was of course not exclusively, or even primarily, concerned with land. Far from it. One of the many features of royal government which made the kingdom of England so precocious was its extensive corpus of royal legislation. This was professedly elaborated on the basis of the royal law codes of the kingdoms which had existed prior to the conquest and unification of England by the kings of Wessex during the late 9th and 10th centuries. Some of these survive. This legislation deals with all manner of topics in great detail, but they say very little about land. Old English land law has largely to be inferred from other sources. William the Conqueror tried to present himself as a pukka English king in the legislative, as in every other, sense. Those fragments of his legislation which survive are drafted in writs, rather than codes. But they are all presented as traditional: legislating by writ was an Old English development, albeit a recent one. King William's extant legislation, too, says almost nothing about land law. Rather, it focuses on regulating relations between conquerors and conquered, a traditional problem in a kingdom which had suffered extensive Viking settlement, and eventually, in the early 11th century, conquest by Cnut, king of Denmark. Just as the *status quo* under Edward the Confessor rapidly became the touchstone for the definition of legitimate tenure, so what was termed the law of Edward the Confessor was what William claimed he was simply reaffirming—even if he admitted that he was occasionally obliged to supplement it with 'additions which I have decreed for the utility of the English people'.

Sometimes the practicalities of conquest and military occupation forced him to innovate, despite the strenuous professions of continuity. For obvious reasons, this was especially true in the early days, when Englishmen in whose craw the Conquest stuck still flailed ineffectually against it. Not every problem could be solved by brutal repression. Allowing Exeter to capitulate on favourable terms in 1068, despite its initial defiance of the king, served to break the coalition between the city and the sons of King Harold. Ingenuity could prove more effective than savagery in other circumstances. Thus, in order to discourage insurgent assassination of Frenchmen, a massive fine was imposed upon the local community if a corpse was discovered and it could not be proven to be that of an Englishman. The aim was clearly to discourage the recalcitrant English from taking potshots at any passing Frenchman. But even in this instance, the *murdrum* fine, as it was called, was ingeniously devised using relevant materials from Old English law. Existing English laws could be exploited in order to create something necessary and new, which could also be presented as traditional. They provided the Conqueror with a ready-made resource of applied legal principles, with a patina of impeccable Englishness. There was no conflict between practical necessity and theory. Rather, there was a characteristically Norman congruence between them.

The claim to continuity with Edward the Confessor's England was intrinsic to the justification of William's conquest, and therefore to its legal and tenurial consequences. Many of those consequences were obvious to contemporaries, but the connection with William's claim to the throne was not. The most perceptive observer—an English monk called Eadmer, who wrote a *History of Novelties* in Canterbury at the start of the 12th century—saw that the system of tenure had been transformed by the Conqueror, and that, by contrast with Old English practice, 'everything, divine and human alike, waited on [the king's] nod'. He did not directly refute William's claim, perhaps because it would still have been imprudent to do so. Instead he satirized it, by reinterpreting many of the familiar details and blending them into an account which was even more improbable than the official story.

That story is preserved in most detail by William of Poitiers. Eadmer's fanciful irreverence was unprecedented, and daring enough. Perhaps because he mocked Duke William's claim, he failed to grasp the connection between it and the tenurial transformation. He thought that the Conqueror had simply imported the new system, ready made, from Normandy. Thereby he vastly overestimated the powers of the duke, who had not been the source of all tenure in this small, primitive principality on the western extremity of the French kingdom. William had no equivalent 'nod' as duke.

But if Eadmer misunderstood the source of the Conqueror's 'nod', he had nevertheless identified the fundamental 'novelty' of the Conquest. Perhaps because the careful preservation of English institutions and governmental practices lent some credence to the façade of continuity, other observers failed to put their fingers on precisely how conquered England was so quickly so different from what had preceded it. Eadmer's perspicuity was unique, as William of Malmesbury, the other great early 12th-century historian of England, acknowledged, in a rare compliment. But if other commentators lacked Eadmer's insight, even the most myopic could hardly fail to notice the changes which had overwhelmed the kingdom, some of which sprang from the novelty which Eadmer had identified as fundamental. Many of the consequences of the Conquest were less abstract and insidious, and therefore more obvious, than the connection between claims to continuity with Edward the Confessor's England and the king's powers over the tenure of land.

For instance, within fifty years of 1066 every English cathedral church and most major abbeys had been razed to the ground, and rebuilt in a new continental style, known to architects as 'Romanesque'. The term was coined only in 1819, to convey the style's imperfect aping of ancient Roman architecture, particularly in its adoption of round arches. In a very literal sense, this rebuilding was one aspect of the renewal of the English church to which Duke William appears to have pledged himself early in 1066, in order to secure papal backing for the Conquest. No English cathedral retains any masonry above ground which dates from before the Conquest. Wulfstan, bishop of Worcester, was the only English bishop to survive the wholesale renewal (or, differently expressed, purge) of the English hierarchy during the first decade of the reign, and its replacement with prelates of continental—chiefly Norman—extraction. He was said to have wept as he watched the demolition of the old cathedral church at Worcester: 'We wretches destroy the work of the saints, thinking in our insolent pride that we are improving them...How many holy and devout men have served God in this place!' He was not simply giving voice to nostalgia. To an Englishman, it seems, a church was itself a relic, sanctified by those who had once worshipped in it. Wulfstan's regret was that improvement now tended to be measured in architectural, not spiritual, terms. 'We strive to pile up stones while neglecting souls.' According to him, true renewal meant recovering the spiritual purity of those who had built the old church long ago, in the 10th century. Building works might become an illusory, materialistic substitute. But he did not high-mindedly oppose the rebuilding, necessitated at least in part by an expansion of the reinvigorated monastic community at Worcester. Indeed, he made a substantial contribution to the decoration of the new church. His pious lament was a pose. The sinuous, self-interested pragmatism of this uniquely successful English vicar of Bray prevailed.

Where the bishop or abbot of Edward the Confessor's reign did not survive—which is to say, very soon in almost every other major church—the newly installed continental prelates embarked on a programme of systematic rebuilding with as much zeal as they cleared out the Augean stable of relics of alleged English saints. Indeed, these were two aspects of the same process of physical renewal. Only those saints whose sanctity could be documented to the satisfaction of the new brooms stood any chance of translation into shrines in the new churches. Lanfranc, the Conqueror's appointment as archbishop of Canterbury, was a stickler in this respect. Frenchmen assessed the legitimacy, as it were, of English saints, and found many woefully wanting. They were consigned to the dustbin of history. Warin, abbot of Malmesbury, piled up the relics of many local saints 'like a heap of rubbish, or the remains of worthless hirelings, and threw them out of the church door'. He even mocked them: '"Now", he said, "let the most powerful of them come to the aid of the rest!"' Paul, the new abbot of St Albans and Lanfranc's nephew, destroyed the tombs of former abbots, whom he described as 'yokels and idiots', and even refused to transfer to the new church the body of the abbey's founder, King Offa of Mercia.

The relics of the exceptional ones who made the unforgiving Norman grade were often translated into the new buildings on their feast days. Thus St Swithun was removed from the Old Minster, Winchester, on 15 July 1093, and installed in the newly completed eastern end of the cathedral, which had been started by Bishop Walkelin in 1079. Demolition of the Old Minster began on the following day 'by order of Bishop Walkelin'. Within a year only 'one chapel [*porticus*] and the high altar' were left of the church in which Edward the Confessor had been crowned and many members of the Old English royal house had been buried. Their remains too were removed to the new cathedral which stood in its place: as the Old Minster was demolished, the nave of the new cathedral was extended westwards over its site. The cathedral therefore even disregarded well-established conventions for rebuilding by failing to respect the axis of the Old Minster. When complete, Winchester Cathedral was the longest church in Europe. Unlike Old English churches, Old English saints were not systematically eliminated. But in the process of evaluation and selective translation, those who were permitted to survive were sanitized and appropriated by the new hierarchy. In this way, they were made to lend their authority, as it were, to the pretence that nothing had changed. In truth, of course, Old England, in an architectural sense, had been eradicated.

1. Winchester Cathedral from the west. The outline of the Old Minster, which was demolished to make way for it, is marked out on the ground

This is true not only of churches. As part of the process of subjugating a conquered country where the natives remained restive, and, for the first decade, intermittently rebellious, scores of castles were constructed. Like the *murdrum* fine, they are testimony to the imperatives of military occupation. Unlike ecclesiastical buildings, with castles there could be no pretence at continuity. True, a very few of these foreign-style fortifications had been built in England during Edward the Confessor's reign, on the Welsh marches. But they were so new-fangled that there was no English word for them. With the Conquest, castles

13

immediately began to spring up. The Bayeux Tapestry depicts a rudimentary one being constructed at Hastings even before the battle. In Winchester, William fitzOsbern, the Conqueror's steward and his most trusted lieutenant, began building a castle between Christmas 1066, when Duke William was crowned king, and February 1067. Whole streets of the existing city were demolished to make way for it. Although this castle was a particularly important one, because of Winchester's role as the kingdom's main governmental centre, in this respect Winchester was no different from those in other major towns. The sheriff, as the king's local representative, ran the shire from the new castle. Before 1069, Sheriff Urse d'Abetôt raised a castle in Worcester which, with characteristic Norman insensitivity, encroached on the cemetery of the cathedral monks. In this instance, even Wulftsan's unctuousness failed to protect his church. The extent of the destruction throughout the kingdom is emphatic testimony to the brutal efficiency with which the Conqueror imposed himself on England. With the simultaneous construction of new cathedral or abbey churches—frequently both—anything up to half the area of existing towns and cities was redeveloped in this way.

The new Norman buildings have for so long been so central to the image of England that it is almost impossible to conceive of them as quite unfamiliar foreign excrescences. But that is how they must have looked to natives. English towns were to know nothing as systematic again until the Blitz and post war reconstruction, or the 1960s. Even these later episodes of substantial urban redevelopment fail to match the scale, as they lack the taste, of the Norman one. They also lack its overriding colonial rationale: the parallel which springs to mind is the cities of the Raj. Moreover, the Norman rebuilding which began in the towns spread out into the countryside. According to the early 12th-century historian Orderic Vitalis, whose mother had been English, but who wrote in Normandy, new Norman lords took pride in building—often rebuilding—parish churches in the new style, alongside 'fortifications which the Normans call *castella*, which were hardly known in some parts of England'. In a physical sense, the Normans reconstructed England in their own image. It must soon have been difficult to remember what Old England had looked like. An Englishman who had left the country in 1066 and returned in, say, 1100 would have found much of it literally unrecognizable. That, of course, was the point.

The desire to preserve the memory of Old England before it was irretrievably lost was one of Eadmer's main motives for writing history. Like his admirer William of Malmesbury, he carefully documented the lives of several English saints, mainly of the late 10th century, which he, like Wulfstan of Worcester (whose *Life* William of Malmesbury wrote, on the basis of a now lost life written in Old English), seemed to regard as England's golden age. If the evidence was clearly recorded, reforming Norman prelates could be persuaded to accept the authenticity of these saints. He and William of Malmesbury also shared an interest in architecture. In two books, Eadmer recorded details of the layout of the old cathedral complex at Canterbury, much of which had burnt down in 1067, and the rest of which had been demolished in 1070. In his *Miracles of St Dunstan*, he did so in the context of an eye-witness account of the translations out of the ruins of the relics of Dunstan and Ælfeah, two Canterbury saints who passed muster with Archbishop Lanfranc. Such memories were to be cherished. There was perhaps a comfort in recording the precise empirical detail: Eadmer makes it clear in his *Life of Dunstan* that he had visited Glastonbury Abbey to inspect Dunstan's cell there, and gives its exact dimensions. By the time of writing, it would also almost certainly have been demolished, because the Norman Abbot Thurstan (1077–1100) had begun to rebuild the church (and, in an infamous atrocity, imposed a new, continental liturgy by force, with three recalcitrant monks being slain by his men-at-arms on the high altar, 'so that the blood came from the altar on to the steps, and from the steps on to the floor').

Eadmer's first books were saints' lives; but, as already mentioned, in the early 12th century he expanded his horizons to write a *History of Novelties*. This focused on Eadmer's own community, Christ Church, Canterbury; but because of Canterbury's unique role, as the see of the archbishop and self-proclaimed primate of all the churches of Britain, it perforce concerned itself not just with local interests, but with the whole kingdom. As such, it took a first step towards filling the gap in English historical writing which, as William of Malmesbury would soon point out, had opened up in the early 8th century with the death of Bede, the first historian to describe the English as a people. For almost four hundred years there appeared to have been very little historical writing in England, other than the rudimentary vernacular annals now known collectively as the *Anglo-Saxon Chronicle*. Eadmer makes it clear that what prompted him to step into this breach was the Conquest, which, in his view, constituted an Old Testament-style divine punishment, inflicted on the English for their sins. It marked a major rupture in English history.

As his title suggests, he devoted most of his attention to recent, post-Conquest developments. He was concerned primarily with the consequences of the Conquest. Those who followed his lead, however—the most notable being William of Malmesbury— concentrated primarily on the period prior to 1066. They sought to mend (in William's felicitous metaphor) the 'chain' which had been broken at Bede's death, and to re-connect Norman England with what had preceded it. Their achievement was to make the second quarter of the 12th century one of the great periods of English historical writing about England. The archival research and the overall framework established by William of Malmesbury, Henry of Huntingdon—whose analysis was more straightforward and therefore more influential—and a number of lesser historians, shaped the way in which medieval English history was understood thereafter. It still does.

While acknowledging the Conquest as the most dramatic rupture in England's history, they fitted it into a sequence of earlier conquests by Romans, Angles and Saxons, Vikings, and Danes. Thereby they re-established the continuity of English history. They were able to do so only by accepting, by and large, the truth of the claim that underpinned the official doctrine of continuity with Edward the Confessor's England. William of Malmesbury ties himself up in knots trying (and failing) to fit all the details into a coherent story. Eadmer satirizes it. Neither of them overtly challenges it. If Norman England was going to be reconnected with pre-Conquest England, they had nothing else to put in its place. There was no alternative, English story—or at least none appears to have survived in writing. In that sense, William the Conqueror's appropriation of the past had ensured his control not just of the present, but of the future. Eadmer, who was English, and William of Malmesbury and Henry of Huntingdon, who were both half English, might insinuate with the subtlety of those Roman historians they so admired that the Conquest had been the rape of England. But however successful they were in restoring its integrity by unearthing information about Old England, they could not undermine the transformation in English tenure, law, ecclesiastical life, and architecture, much of which flowed from the claim to continuity on which they, too, had to depend in order to explain why the Conquest had taken place.

The slower transformation in the English language, which had virtually ceased to be used for writing by the mid-12th century, cannot be linked directly to the same cause. But these historians all revealed that they were acutely aware of the problems which arose in a society in which three languages—English, French, and Latin—were in simultaneous oral use. (William of Malmesbury comments waspishly on the howlers in Old English perpetrated by another historian of purely Norman extraction.) Moreover, it is a fact worth pondering that the first surviving book to be written in French was a history of the English, written for

Constance fitzGilbert, the wife of a Lincolnshire tenant-in-chief, in the 1130s. Lincolnshire can be bleak and boring, and doubtless diversions were required to while away the long evenings. But it is remarkable that second-generation aristocratic French settlers could find this sort of thing entertaining. Gaimar's *Histoire des Engleis* amounts to over 6,000 lines, in verse, most of which are concerned with pre-Conquest English history, based on a version of the *Anglo-Saxon Chronicle* which Gaimar claimed to have consulted in Winchester (where a chained copy had, his audience learned, been provided for a curious public by King Alfred).

The very profundity of the changes wrought so quickly by the Conquest meant that lay Norman colonists could, by the early 12th century, begin in some sense to identify with English history, even if they had to do so in French. By then, within the span of a single lifetime, there is no indication that anyone any longer wanted to reverse those changes, or even had much conception of what Old England had really been like. That is the scale and character of the 'regime change' imposed on the kingdom of England in 1066.

Chapter 1
William's coronation

On the day fixed for the coronation, the archbishop of York, a
great lover of justice and a man of mature years, wise, good, and
eloquent, addressed the English, and asked them in a fitting address
whether they would consent to [Duke William] being crowned
as their lord. They all shouted their joyful assent without any
hesitation, as if heaven had granted them a single mind and a single
voice. The Normans most readily re-echoed the wish of the English,
after the bishop of Coutances had inquired as to their opinion. But
others who had been posted as an armed, mounted guard around
the monastery, on hearing the loud clamour in an unknown tongue,
decided that something sinister was afoot, and imprudently torched
the city roundabout.

Thus does William of Poitiers, biographer (and chaplain) of Duke
William of Normandy, describe the consummation of the Norman
conquest of England: William's coronation as king in Westminster
Abbey, on Christmas Day 1066. It was at this precise point that
Duke William at last received the kingdom which, according
to the Norman claim already elaborated by William of Poitiers,
King Edward the Confessor had bequeathed to him long before.
That the description of the coronation ceremony is so detailed
reflects its key role in the realization of Duke William's claim to
succeed Edward as king. Normans were unaccustomed to royal
ceremonial, because their ruler was a mere duke. Evidently they

were impressed by the novelty of the spectacle, and struck by the way in which it transformed him. The English members of the congregation, facing the tomb in which Edward had been interred within a few days of celebrating the consecration of his newly completed abbey church the previous Christmas, were said to have voluntarily and unanimously accepted William as king. Yet even at this triumphant climax in William of Poitiers' eulogy—in which the duke had repeatedly been compared to an earlier invader of England, Julius Caesar, though always to the latter's detriment—he felt it necessary to admit that there had been a regrettable glitch. Sentries had been posted around the church, presumably to protect William from any rogue Englishmen who were still inclined to resist his accession as king. They had been so alarmed by the sounds of joyful, if guttural, acclamation within, that they had set fire to neighbouring buildings.

William of Poitiers' account was written in Normandy about ten years after the event—certainly by 1077. According to Orderic Vitalis, a monastic historian from the Norman abbey of St-Évroult who used and embellished William of Poitiers' book in the 1120s, this incident had left the new king 'trembling from head to foot'. His foreboding was justified: the conflagration turned out to be a 'portent of future catastrophes'; henceforth 'the English never again trusted the Normans'. Given his half-English descent, he probably felt well-qualified to comment. Orderic, unlike his source, dwelt on this ominous event, rather than passing over it briskly. But he did not, at least not explicitly, point out the absurdity of William of Poitiers' explanation. A tense armed guard, startled by apparent uproar within the church, would surely have rushed inside in order to protect their duke. It would have been so easy to do so, because the west end was still incomplete, and may have been open to the elements. They would certainly not have rampaged in the opposite direction, burning buildings as they went. Orderic, who had been born in England and was half English, intermittently expresses some sympathy for the subjugated people. His account here may be a subtle case in point, for he states that the congregation were so alarmed by the uproar around the church that they rushed outside 'in frantic haste', some to fight the flames, others to loot. By implication, but only by implication, the firefighters were English and the looters Norman. If so, the explicit explanation, adopted from William of Poitiers, for the motives of the fire-raising Norman sentries is undermined, and a more credible one suggested: the Norman troops were not jumpy bodyguards who had responded in an utterly irrational fashion when startled by an unexpected din. Rather, they were members of a conquering army who proved incapable of restraining themselves from arson and plundering even at the very moment when their duke was formally acceding to the rightful inheritance for which, supposedly, they had all fought. Their comrades-in-arms inside the church behaved in exactly the same way as soon as the disorder outside afforded them the pretext to desert their new king, at the very moment when he was becoming king, in order to satisfy their lust for booty. In covertly subverting William of Poitiers' brazenly implausible special pleading in this way, Orderic subtly juxtaposed the scrupulous legalism with which the Norman Conquest was justified—William's claim to his rightful inheritance—with its brutal concupiscence. As Orderic perceived, so far as Duke William, his co-conquerors, and above all his apologists were concerned, these two aspects of the Conquest were inseparable.

The anonymous author of the only manuscript of the vernacular *Anglo-Saxon Chronicle* still being written by the time of King William's death in 1087—known to modern scholars as the E version, or Peterborough chronicle—encapsulated the point in an epigram: 'The more loudly just law was talked about, the more unlawful things were done.' He makes clear that he was not just an obscure English monk casting an embittered eye back over the events of the reign from some distant cloister; he had himself lived at William's court, and had often 'looked upon him'. He knew the new regime from the inside, like William of Poitiers. He comments, for instance, on the new king's passion for English

2. William of Jumièges presents his history of the Norman dukes to William the Conqueror, from the initial letter of his dedicatory epistle. This copy—Rouen, Bibliothèque municipale MS. 1174 (714) fo. 116—is the autograph of Orderic Vitalis' early twelfth-century reworking of the history

royal ceremony: 'he was very dignified: three times every year he wore his crown, as often as he was in England'. But unlike William of Poitiers, the author of the E version was no spin doctor. He did not feel impelled to protest too much, as William of Poitiers did, that he 'never took a single step beyond the truth'. He offers what appears to be a more balanced, as well as a more lapidary, assessment of the reign. Much of it serves to undermine the near contemporary Norman *encomia* by William of Poitiers and (c. 1071) William of Jumièges, who is depicted in one manuscript presenting a copy of his book to the king. Whereas William of Poitiers emphasizes that the king gave 'nothing to any Gaul which had been unjustly taken from any Englishman', the English annalist reported, in verse, that everyone

> ...had to follow out the king's will entirely
> If they wished to live or hold their land,
> Property or estate, or his favour great.

Or as Henry of Huntingdon, an English near-contemporary of Orderic, summed up the doleful message of the *Anglo-Saxon Chronicle*, his main source: 'It was an insult then even to be called English.' If Orderic was right to say that English resentment of the Normans sprang from the plundering and rapine in London on Christmas Day 1066, then it had, as the authors of all the versions of the *Anglo-Saxon Chronicle* lamented, flourished exceedingly during the ensuing reign.

But Orderic's description of events prior to the coronation makes it abundantly clear that hostility between English and Normans had already been deeply rooted well before that fateful day. Most obviously, the English had fought and lost a pitched battle against Duke William's forces near Hastings, and a series of subsequent rearguard actions (including one in an 'open space' in London shortly before the coronation, according to William of Jumièges). William of Poitiers, Orderic's chief source, reveals that English hostility to Normans was amply reciprocated by the time he wrote.

William's narrative is sprinkled with bitter aspersions against the English: according to this Frenchman, the English were already a notoriously perfidious lot. Orderic's evaluation of the consequence of the arson which accompanied the coronation was, as he said, a portent; it was not meant to be taken literally. It was designed to underscore the definitive significance which the coronation had had for Normans from the very beginning, as demonstrated by the fact that for Normans this, and not victory at Hastings, or the submission at Berkhamsted, was what made William king.

This Norman understanding of coronation was quite at variance with English tradition. Previously English kings had been created by recognition (or 'election'), which had in some cases (including Edward the Confessor's) happened a year or more prior to coronation. From William the Conqueror's accession, a candidate would, by contrast, become king only when anointed during the coronation ceremony. Accordingly, coronation became a much more urgent priority for a new king than it had been in Old England. But this was not the only difference between Norman and English perceptions of the significance of the central and (as William of Poitiers reveals) pre-ordained event of Christmas Day 1066. This is suggested by contemporary or near-contemporary English accounts.

A manuscript of the *Anglo-Saxon Chronicle* known to modern scholars as D, which petered out in 1079, contains a detailed account of William's coronation. This version of the *Chronicle* has been shown to have been written during this period by a member of Archbishop Ealdred of York's household. It is, therefore, the closest we are ever going to get to an eye-witness account of the event, and it deserves to be taken very seriously. It records that William 'promised Ealdred on Christ's book and swore moreover (before Ealdred would place the crown on his head) that he would rule all this people as the best of kings before him, if they would be loyal to him'. It strongly suggests that the officiating archbishop extracted promises of good conduct from

William as a precondition for coronation. In this respect, it fitted in with Old English tradition, which preserves a lot of evidence for kings, at their coronations, promising to rule well, although none for those promises being a precondition for receiving the crown. That the promises were conditional on the loyalty of the subjects was also traditional, although coronation promises seem never previously to have been framed in these terms. Rather, the conditional nature of William's promises echoes almost verbatim undertakings which King Cnut of Denmark, the early 11th-century conqueror of England, had given to the newly subjugated English in an initial proclamation. And he in turn was echoing what Edgar, the late 10th-century king, had offered to the Scandinavian settlers in areas over which he had recently asserted English control. Whether or not anything of the kind was integrated into the coronation ceremony for William the Conqueror in 1066, it is clear that the member of Archbishop Ealdred's household who wrote up this account was well aware of relevant English precedents. He considered that they had been adapted to the particular circumstances of the Conquest.

Much of this account is reproduced in an early 12th-century Latin chronicle written at Worcester by a monk called John, which had probably been commissioned by Bishop Wulfstan as part of the Worcester historiographical drive to preserve the records of Old England. It was clearly based on a lost version of the *Anglo-Saxon Chronicle* close to D; but unlike D, John supplies a text for the promises. He found it in a pontifical, a bishop's liturgical handbook, possibly in Worcester Cathedral library. In other words, he felt the need to amplify the *Chronicle's* account by reference to the liturgical format for a coronation, although the one he chose could not possibly have been used in 1066. However, neither John of Worcester, nor any surviving manuscript of the *Anglo-Saxon Chronicle*, says anything at all about the acclamation on which William of Poitiers laid so much emphasis. Conversely, William of Poitiers says nothing about royal promises. The perspectives of near contemporary Norman and English commentators were almost entirely distinct. The possible liturgical formats for the event, preserved in pontificals, suggest that there would have been promises and perhaps also an acclamation; but they do not confirm that either feature would have taken the particular form on which so much stress is laid in the respective English and Norman accounts of the events of Christmas Day 1066. They are not incompatible; both may be accurate, if very partial, records of events on the crucial day. But they are revealing of the distance between English and Norman perceptions and interpretations. The coronation is an instructive example of the difficulties inherent in trying to establish, on the basis of sources written from such different perspectives, precisely what might have happened.

William's claim

What is true of the ceremonial beginning of the reign is *a fortiori* the case with the claim which that coronation consummated. For although some of the details of the coronation are agreed between the English and Norman accounts, there is no contemporary English corroboration at all for the Norman justification of the Conquest. Yet that justification, details of which are repeated over and over again by the otherwise terse William of Jumièges, and elaborated with such painstaking legalistic precision by William of Poitiers, is the key to understanding how the Conquest was implemented and therefore to many of its most important consequences. Duke William's claim provided the template for the Conquest. What was it, and why did contemporary English sources seem quite unaware of it?

Most of it was perforce concerned with events which had allegedly taken place in Edward the Confessor's reign, for it sprang from a decision allegedly made by Edward in the early 1050s. According to William of Poitiers, King Edward had decided that he wanted the young duke of Normandy, the grandson of his mother's brother, Duke Richard II, to succeed him as king. He had, therefore, summoned an assembly of the English nobility, and had apparently made each individual take an oath to accept Duke William as king after his death. These oaths had been sworn in William's absence. News of the designation was communicated to Duke William in Normandy by Robert of Jumièges, the former Norman abbot whom Edward had recently translated from the see of London to Canterbury. This detail suggests that the event took place sometime in 1051, when Robert of Jumièges was promoted to Canterbury. It is referred to four times; the most detailed account, placed in the mouth of Duke William just prior to the battle of Hastings, records the names of four of the most prominent oath takers. Unaccountably, Harold, eldest son of Godwine, earl of Wessex, and himself at this point earl of East Anglia, is missing from this list. But at some time in 1064 or 1065 (again the internal chronology is vague) Harold, who had by this point become earl of Wessex in succession to his father, was sent by the king to Normandy in order to reaffirm the existing arrangement. There Harold had 'sworn fidelity to [William] according to the holy rite of Christians'; it is stressed that Edward had arranged this in order that Harold, uniquely, should swear in person to the duke what his father and others had sworn in William's absence. 'Many of the most distinguished and truthful men who were there as witnesses' had testified to the oath, the self-proclaimed truth-teller relates. Harold had pledged his faith with his hand resting on a reliquary; Duke William fought at Hastings with these relics suspended around his neck. In more rudimentary form, William of Jumièges tells much the same story, and reiterates the terms of Harold's oath three times over, despite his normal tendency to terseness.

The terms of that oath, more scrupulously detailed by William of Poitiers, meant that Harold was uniquely obliged to aid and abet Duke William in succeeding to the kingdom to which Edward had made him heir. Sometimes William of Poitiers gives the impression that the English as a people had been bound too, as if the individual nobles who swore in 1051 or 1052, or perhaps Harold in 1064 or 1065, had somehow acted not just on their own account, but vicariously, on behalf of the people as a whole. Whether William of Poitiers thought that this was the case or not, in the event Harold claimed that the king, as he lay dying, had chosen to bequeath the kingdom instead to Harold. Harold, denounced as a perjurer by William of Poitiers, had 'seized the royal throne' on the following day, when Edward was interred in the new abbey church at Westminster. Harold had been anointed by Stigand, archbishop of Canterbury, the only surviving one of those identified as having sworn in 1051 or 1052 to accept William as Edward's successor. Stigand was not legitimately archbishop, because he had usurped the position from Robert of Jumièges, Edward's Norman appointee. As a usurper, he had been 'deprived of priestly ministry by the just zeal and authority of the pope'. As a consequence, in William of Poitiers' view, Stigand's rushed anointing of Harold was invalid. Not only had Harold previously barred himself from accepting the bequest allegedly made by the dying Edward, his own status as king was doubly compromised, because the coronation which, in William of Poitiers' view, made a king, had been conducted by someone incapable of administering the anointing. One usurper had anointed another. The notoriously perfidious English had in Harold a king whose very status as king was proof of his perfidy.

The various versions of the *Anglo-Saxon Chronicle* are fuller for the reign of Edward the Confessor than for any other Old English king, including Alfred. They are not always consistent with each other as to details, and often gnomically random in a way which makes it almost impossible to distinguish the significant detail from the inconsequential. But their differences in perspective suggest that the annals were being written up contemporaneously and fitfully, in different locations, and that there was no single, official line which the various annalists felt obliged to reproduce. Not only do they lack the consistency of William of Jumièges and William of Poitiers, they also, being contemporary, lack the teleological hindsight of the Norman accounts. None of these versions corroborates in any way the story retailed by William of Jumièges and William of Poitiers. (There is one arguable and partial exception: the E version of the *Anglo-Saxon Chronicle* records that Robert of Jumièges went abroad in 1051, though it states that he went to Rome, to collect his archiepiscopal *pallium*, not to Normandy, to notify William that he had been designated as the next king of England.) Nor does the biography of King Edward, commissioned by his queen, the writing of which was overtaken by the catastrophe of conquest. Historians have tried to bend the evidence to establish some common ground between the English and Norman sources, but in truth there is none. Furthermore, in some respects the English sources are almost impossible to reconcile with that Norman story, although historians have been trying to reconcile them ever since the early 12th century.

For instance, King Edward, who was childless, arranged in the mid-1050s to recall to England from Hungarian exile the last two male descendants of the West Saxon (or English) royal line: the son of his half-brother, King Edmund Ironside, also named Edward, and Edward's young son, Edgar. Both were *æthelings*, that is to say, male descendants of kings of the originally West Saxon house of Cerdic. Edmund Ironside had succumbed to Cnut, and his son Edward *ætheling* had fled to Hungary to escape the Danish conqueror, just as his half-brothers Edward and Alfred had fled to Normandy. There could have been only one reason for arranging their return: as potential successors to Edward. But if Edward had already nominated Duke William to succeed him, and had gone to the lengths described by William of Poitiers in order to ensure that his wish would be realized, then to change his mind in this way would indicate that the king was fickle to the point of promiscuity where the succession to his throne was concerned. The D version of the *Chronicle* records that Edward *ætheling* died almost immediately on arrival in England in 1057: 'we do not know for what reason it was brought about that he was not allowed to see [the face?] of his kinsman King Edward'. The implication that there was something rotten in the kingdom of England under Edward the Confessor, without divulging any definite information, is characteristically cryptic—an impression strengthened by the mysterious syntactical gap in the surviving text, filled by the conjectural reading in square brackets. The *ætheling*'s son, Edgar—also, by definition, an *ætheling*—survived at the royal court. But he was not treated as *æthelings* had traditionally been: he did not, for instance, attest any of Edward the Confessor's charters, whereas *æthelings* customarily attested at the very top of the witness list, even as infants. Edgar was not accorded this prominent, official recognition of his (by then) unique status. Moreover, he held none of the estates customarily reserved for *æthelings*. His father may or may not have been summarily dispatched in 1057; he had certainly been sidelined soon afterwards.

There can be no doubt that the king's relatives did return to England in 1057. But their return made little sense if Edward had already arranged for Duke William to be king after him. William of Poitiers affected to know a great deal about the events of Edward the Confessor's reign, but he makes no allusion to this one, which had massive implications for the case he was expounding. All he does is acknowledge the existence of Edgar '*Athelinus*' (Latinizing the English title, despite his distaste for neologisms) after the battle of Hastings. So when William of Malmesbury, writing in the 1120s, attempted to wrestle with this conflict of evidence, he suggested that Edward had bequeathed England to William only after the death of his nephew Edward *ætheling*. This imposed some logical sense on the records of events (though it simply overlooked Edgar *ætheling*, whom William of Malmesbury had previously mentioned), but only by asserting what no source said, and distorting the chronology of the Norman accounts in order to make them compatible with the English ones. In that respect, his reconstruction is not unlike the modern hypothesis that Earl Harold arranged the return of the *æthelings* from Hungary. The king could not have done so, the argument runs, because he had already committed himself to Duke William.

It must therefore have been Harold who wanted the *æthelings* back, in order to sabotage that arrangement. This is an hypothesis for which there is no evidence whatsoever. As in the case of William of Malmesbury's rearrangement of chronology, it suggests that the English and Norman accounts of the reign of Edward the Confessor can only be reconciled by selectively ignoring events they record, or by distorting them, or by making up events for which no source provides any warrant. Or rather, this is the case up to the death of King Edward, at which point both sets of sources start to recount what are recognizably the same events, if from very different perspectives, and with significant discrepancies. That this is the case from 5 January 1066, but is manifestly not so prior to that date, despite the profusion of detail about Edward's reign in the two categories of source, renders that absence of any agreement whatsoever (other than Archbishop Robert of Jumièges' trip abroad, explained in quite different ways) all the more striking.

Modern historians have not progressed far beyond the welter of confusion, contradiction, special pleading, and willful disregard of inconvenient evidence in which William of Malmesbury's account of Duke William's claim eventually collapsed. He was so baffled by conflicting suggestions that Harold had been sent to Normandy by the king, and conversely (according to Eadmer) that Harold had disobeyed a strict royal prohibition against his going, that he ended up suggesting that Harold had been on a fishing trip, and that his boat had been blown off course. Harold's visit to Normandy had therefore simply been an unfortunate and unforeseen accident. This explanation, for which there is of course no evidence either, is testimony to no more than William of Malmesbury's desperation in the face of irreconcilable pieces of evidence.

We can eschew such desperation by taking a different approach. It was William of Poitiers who compared the Normans at the battle of Hastings to orators in a judicial plea. If we treat the Norman claim not as verifiable history, but rather as a legal argument, then it is no longer necessary to make painful efforts at reconciliation with the contemporary English sources. As with any legal argument, the claim would certainly involve the tendentious interpretation, calculated disregard, and perhaps even the fabrication, of evidence. But like all legal arguments, it would have been constructed in accordance with an accepted legal framework which, precisely because it was accepted, would require little, if any, explicit elucidation. In this case, that framework would, or should, be the customary conventions of succession. Did Duke William's claim comply with the traditions of arranging royal succession in England?

It must be admitted at the outset that English royal succession in the 11th century had already been grievously disrupted by the Danish conquest, completed by King Cnut in 1016–18. But Cnut's longest surviving son, the childless King Harthacnut, appears to have pre-arranged a restoration of the English royal line by inviting Edward the Confessor back from exile in Normandy, much as the childless Edward would later, as king, invite his male relatives back from Hungary. By the time Edward received Harthacnut's summons, he was the eldest surviving son of King Æthelred 'the Unready', and therefore the oldest *ætheling*. He duly became king on Harthacnut's death in 1042. But other than this unprecedented restoration of the line of Cerdic, there is little evidence that English kings in the 10th and 11th centuries had any choice over who should succeed them, prior to Edward's well-attested selection of Earl Harold, who was anomalous precisely because he was not of the line of Cerdic. When King Æthelred had died in 1016, Edmund Ironside, his eldest surviving son, and therefore senior *ætheling*, was straightforwardly accepted as king in his stead. There is no suggestion that he had been in some way formally nominated by his father, or recognized by the nobility prior to his father's death. The story, told in the biography of Edward the Confessor, that Edward had received oaths from English nobles while still in his mother's womb, is obviously designed to establish that his ultimate succession as king had always been providentially ordained, despite the fact that he was Æthelred's sixth son. It is also avowedly based on an Old Testament model—Jeremiah i, 5—rather than on English practice.

Historians have offered learned disquisitions on the relative strengths of deathbed (or *verba novissima*) bequests as opposed to earlier (or *post obitum*) arrangements, as if these practices were relevant to English royal succession in 1066. Duke William, it is argued, had received a *post obitum* gift from King Edward, confirmed by the oaths of the nobility, and Earl Harold a *verba novissima* one. In Old English custom, a deathbed wish abrogated any prior arrangement. No historian—not even Orderic Vitalis, who made much of this distinction—seems to have paused to reflect that our sole source for this alleged tenet of English testamentary custom is William of Poitiers. William attributes this information to a 'cowled advocate' attempting to make the best case he could for his client, Harold, shortly before the battle of Hastings. The response, dictated by the duke himself to his spokesman, 'a certain monk of Fécamp', and the outcome of the immediately following battle, revealed how valid had been the best case that could have been made for Harold. William of Poitiers assumes his own voice to apostrophize the fallen king: 'Your end demonstrates how rightly you were raised by the gift of Edward at his demise.' King Edward's alleged deathbed bequest of his throne to Harold, recorded with some variations in all versions of the *Anglo-Saxon Chronicle*, and more equivocally in the biography of Edward, is the first evidence for the application of such a practice to royal succession in England. It is, of course, with this event that the pre-Conquest English and post-Conquest Norman sources start to give their very different accounts of what are recognizably the same events.

There is, then, English evidence for a deathbed bequest of the throne in the unprecedented circumstances of January 1066, but none at all for such an event beforehand. Nor is there any English evidence for a *post obitum* bequest of the throne, other than the story told in the Norman sources. Even if we do not judge the near unanimity of the various versions of the *Anglo-Saxon Chronicle* with regard to Edward's deathbed disposition in favour of Harold to be suspiciously overemphatic, why should we accept William of Poitiers as an infallible expert witness on English testamentary custom in general? Furthermore, why should we accept that English testamentary custom was considered relevant to royal succession in England? Yet subsequent historians, from Orderic on, have accepted William of Poitiers' testimony on this subject. It still dominates modern discussions, where it is also accepted unquestioningly.

Just as there is no contemporary English evidence to corroborate the Norman accounts of the events of Edward's reign prior to 5 January 1066, so, it seems, there is none to suggest that succession to the English throne had ever been arranged as Edward the Confessor had allegedly done for Duke William. If that is the case, where did William of Poitiers get the idea from? Once the question is posed, the answer is obvious. William of Jumièges' *Deeds of the Dukes of the Normans* is a sequence of ducal biographies. Shortly before each duke's demise, he is said to have summoned an assembly of his nobles, and to have commanded them to pledge their faith, individually, to his chosen son and successor, in order that each of them should be bound to him prior to his father's death. Anyone who later contested the succession would therefore be guilty of perfidy. William of Jumièges gives no details about the manner in which King Edward originally 'established [William] as heir', but this is exactly the device which William of Poitiers describes being used in England in 1051 or 1052. The only difference is that the English nobles are said to have sworn to Duke William in his absence. Earl Harold, however, had supposedly sworn later, to the duke in person, just as Norman nobles had done to chosen ducal successors since the foundation of the duchy in the early 10th century. According to William of Poitiers, it was for this very purpose that Edward had sent Harold to Normandy. In view of the specific undertakings Harold had given—meticulously itemized by William of Poitiers—his hasty accession as king transformed him into the defining example of English perfidy. What William of Poitiers had done was retrospectively to impose on Edward the Confessor's England the succession practices of the duchy of Normandy. Thereby he both justified Duke William's claim to succeed Edward, and negated Harold's, regardless of the fact that Harold's succession was a *fait accompli*.

To suggest that Edward the Confessor had imported Norman succession practices is frankly incredible. It was one thing for Edward to offer preferment in the English church to continental clerics, or to build churches, like Westminster Abbey, in a new-fangled continental style. It would have been quite another to impose alien, unfamiliar succession practices on the English nobility in an attempt to bind them to an unprecedented royal bequest of the kingdom to an alien. Yet that is what William of Jumièges and William of Poitiers have persuaded most subsequent historians to accept. Whereas the Norman sources feel obliged to acknowledge that Harold had some sort of claim, which they endeavour to refute, the contemporary English sources seem quite unaware of Duke William's claim. Hence the sharp divide between the period from 5 January 1066, when there is some common ground between the two sets of narratives, and the period prior to that date, when there is none. The reason why is quite simply that there was no Norman claim until it was confected in Normandy, on the basis of Norman succession practices. Once the claim is analysed, this is plain.

The simplicity of this solution to the apparent conflict of evidence has not found much favour, because historians have been unwilling to accept that the Norman writers might have reproduced a confected case, or perhaps even confected it themselves. Partly this reluctance arises from an unspoken assumption that medieval monks were simple-minded souls who were doing their inadequate best to record events accurately. Yet it is clear that William of Jumièges and William of Poitiers, or

3. Bayeux Tapestry: the first official, post-Conquest version of what had happened at Harold II's coronation on 6 January 1066

later Orderic Vitalis and William of Malmesbury, wrote with the sophistication, and sometimes the deft obliqueness, insinuation, and evasion of their Roman models.

Moreover, it has been argued that outright mendacity on the part of William of Poitiers and William of Jumièges would have been impossible, even if it were conceivable, because the facts were well known. That they fail to be mentioned in the English sources is deemed to be partly a matter of chance, and partly an expression of a willful English reluctance to face up to them. Yet the modern world, in which communication and therefore knowledge of events is far more widespread, would suggest that this is a very naïve view. The tendentious interpretation of events, and even manifest falsehood, have often been widely accepted precisely because it has been deemed politically necessary that they be accepted. It would have been so much easier to secure such acceptance, at least outwardly, when any sort of knowledge of relevant events was restricted to a very small coterie, rendered much smaller than usual by death in the pitched battles of 1066 and subsequently, by intimidation, and by exile.

A pertinent example is presented by an episode in the Bayeux Tapestry with which we are already familiar: it depicts Stigand presiding at Harold's coronation, as William of Poitiers reports. John of Worcester, however, contradicts this account: he says that Archbishop Ealdred officiated. Perhaps this was what he read in the now lost version of the *Anglo-Saxon Chronicle* very close to D which he used. Yet the D version itself, written in Ealdred's household, records nothing other than the bare fact of Harold's consecration, perhaps because, after the Conquest, it would have been impolitic to draw attention to the role that Ealdred had played in Harold's accession. Moreover, in addition to presenting what is probably a blatantly mendacious image, the captions to other events depicted in the Tapestry seem often deliberately to avoid the point of the pictures they purport to label, as if clear, unambiguous descriptions might have been imprudent. If the Tapestry was designed and produced in England, as seems to be the case, then even more care had to be taken over the phrasing of captions, which tend to be less ambiguous than pictures, and therefore more potentially perilous. The Tapestry was embroidered in a metaphorical, as well as a literal, sense.

From the very start—perhaps even before the start, in view of papal support for the invasion—William the Conqueror's regime was based on an official interpretation of history. This provided the regime's justification. It therefore legitimated the concupiscence which I have already shown Oderic implicitly acknowledging, in his tendentious description of William's coronation, itself derived from William of Poitiers. Scrupulous legalism was based upon a fabricated history, which ultimately legitimated the despoliation of the Conquest. Control of the past was intrinsic to the control of the present, and was understood to be so. William of Poitiers wrote that 'unseemly events necessarily occur in the course of history, and we consider that they should not be deleted from the page, so that such events, in imitation of the original deed, should themselves be deleted'. But in doing so he was yet again pretentiously parading his classical accomplishments, echoing a commonplace of antique historiography, which stressed the need to preserve an accurate record of events for posterity's moral instruction. The heinous event he had in mind was Harold's father's alleged perfidy in arranging the assassination of Edward the Confessor's brother, Alfred *ætheling*, in 1036, shortly after Alfred returned to England. (That Edward *ætheling* died on his return to England in 1057 suggests that returning from exile was not good for the life expectancy of *æthelings* in the 11th century.) William of Poitiers could therefore present perfidious Harold as a chip off the old block, who ultimately paid the price for his father's crime as well as his own.

But if the argument advanced in this chapter be accepted, William was not averse to erasing events from, or indeed inventing and inserting them into, the historical record when necessary. Even events which had undoubtedly occurred, such as William the Conqueror's coronation, were to be massaged and spun in the most brazen and implausible fashion. Immediately after his account of the coronation, he wrote: 'When iniquity reigns, it most often veils its avarice under the pretext of avenging crime, condemning the innocent man to punishment in order to confiscate his possessions.' He did so in order to define by contrast the exemplary justice of the measures taken by the newly crowned King William. But ironically enough, in this particular instance the self-proclaimed truth-teller was telling the truth. (It may have been Orderic's sensitivity to this irony which prompted him to excise this sentence from a passage which otherwise he copied almost verbatim.) William of Poitiers should have known. He had provided the most detailed and influential extant statement of the Conqueror's 'pretext'—or, in the argot of a modern counterpart, he had sexed it up.

But why should so much trouble have been taken over confecting it? After all, there is little sign that Cnut of Denmark in the early 11th century, or Harald Hardrada, king of Norway, who also invaded England in September 1066, devoted anything like this degree of care to formulating a copper-bottomed claim to the English throne. Why was William the Conqueror so extraordinarily scrupulous about justifying the conquest of England? It was this legalistic scrupulosity which necessitated William's control of the past, and which in turn shaped the way in which the Conquest was implemented.

Chapter 2
Papal intervention and the implementation of the Conquest

On one level, the reason why so much care was devoted to the elaboration of Duke William's claim to the kingdom of England is that he had resolved to secure papal backing for his planned invasion. Orderic, amplifying the brief account by William of Poitiers, records that Gilbert fitzOsbern, archdeacon of Lisieux, was sent as ducal ambassador to the papal curia, probably (by implication) sometime early in 1066. (It is curious that William of Poitiers, who at the time of writing was himself archdeacon of Lisieux in succession to Gilbert, fails to identify the ambassador.) Gilbert was a son of William fitzOsbern, who is credited with being the principal advocate of the Conquest and, according to William of Poitiers, 'chief of [Duke William's] army'. Pope Alexander II 'listened to [Gilbert's] account of everything that had taken place, favoured the legitimate duke, ordered him to take up arms boldly against the perjurer, and sent him a banner of St Peter the apostle'. If William fitzOsbern played the crucial role during the battle of Hastings which William of Poitiers attributes to him, then he must have done so close to the banner which his son had brought back from Rome. In 1080, in a letter to King William, Pope Gregory VII recalled the heated debate which Gilbert's arrival had provoked in the curia. Many considered that the pope should not involve himself in sanctioning a war of conquest. Gregory—at the time Hildebrand, archdeacon of the Holy See—had, on the contrary, argued strongly in support of papal intervention. His view had prevailed, despite much 'muttering' among his opponents. If Orderic is to be trusted, Gilbert's account of events was crucial in swaying the curia in favour of the 'legitimate duke' and against the 'perjurer'. In other words, Gilbert must have argued the duke's case in similar terms to those expounded by William of Jumièges and William of Poitiers. Indeed, the resemblances between their repeated recapitulations of the duke's claim suggest that they may have had independent access to a brief similar to Gilbert's, for it is clear that William of Poitiers did not draw directly on William of Jumièges. Since William of Jumièges had finished writing by c. 1071, the brief they both used must have been in existence by that date at the very latest. It had almost certainly been devised by the time the Conquest was launched.

It is likely that this brief was the work of Lanfranc, at the time abbot of Duke William's foundation of St-Étienne, Caen, and, from 1070, archbishop of Canterbury in place of the usurping Stigand. Lanfranc was an accomplished canon lawyer. The closeness of his relationship with the duke reminded William of Poitiers of 'the sweet memory... of the Emperor Theodosius who, when he was about to go into battle against tyrants, was inspired by the prophecies and responses of the monk John...'. Lanfranc probably did more than pronounce 'prophecies' and 'responses' against Harold the tyrant—a term then synonymous with usurper. The case against Harold—that he had usurped the throne, and could therefore not legitimately be king—was in its essentials identical to the case against Stigand, who was deemed to have usurped the archbishopric of Canterbury after the flight of Robert of Jumièges from England in September 1052. That case would have been a particularly powerful one to put to Pope Alexander, who had reiterated the repeated papal condemnations of Stigand, and who was all the more likely to listen attentively to an argument drafted by Lanfranc because Lanfranc had once been his tutor.

At some unspecified point after the Conquest, the pope wrote to King William that Stigand was an 'evil head' whose followers 'burned with the pride of Satan their father'. Together they had 'turned the English people from the path of truth'. Under Stigand's leadership, the English church had rotted from the (evil) head down. When Harold was king, much the same case could be made about the kingdom as a whole. According to William of Poitiers, the duke's 'victory over the tyrant was greatly desired in Rome'. And of course the closely related cases intersected in the (almost certainly mendacious) allegation that Stigand had anointed Harold as king: 'an impious consecration', as William of Poitiers put it. The 'evil head' had consecrated the head of the usurper. The legal authorities to justify this shared case were to be found in Lanfranc's own canon law collection. In his personal copy, some of them are marked for ready reference. It is therefore possible to reconstruct the argument which Pope Alexander endorsed in 1066, and to identify its likely author as the pope's former tutor. But this does not explain why the duke and his principal advisor thought such papal endorsement desirable or necessary.

An obvious reason why they might have sought it, at least to a modern audience, would be to court international opinion. But if that was one of their aims, then the accounts in chronicles written all over late 11th-century Europe, other than in Normandy and Norman-ruled parts of Italy, reveal that papal endorsement was scarcely an unqualified success. For example, 11th-century Flemish chroniclers were unanimous in their condemnation of the Conquest, despite widespread Flemish participation in it. Elsewhere William the Conqueror was often said to have been no more than just that. His dodgy dossier might have hoodwinked the papal curia, by dint of Hildebrand's sterling efforts. But as Wenric of Trier pointedly observed to him in his later incarnation as Pope Gregory, also in 1080, there were rulers who

> having usurped kingdoms by the violence of a tyrant, themselves
> paved the way to the throne with blood, placed a bloodstained
> crown on their heads, and established their rule with murder, rape,
> butchery, and torment; having themselves strangled several close

kinsmen and their lords, they seized their honours; they all call themselves friends of the pope, are honoured by his blessings, and are greeted by him as victorious princes.

The context makes it quite clear whom Wenric had in mind: Gregory's support for the Conqueror had become notorious, and not just among anti-Gregorian polemicists. During the late 11th century, Wenric's view was widely shared. The consensus changed in the 12th century, when Norman rule in England had become an established and unquestionable fact of life; earlier on few seem to have been fooled.

Papal backing failed to persuade most impartial observers of the justice of Duke William's claim, at least in the long term. What it did in the short term, crucially, was to facilitate recruitment of the invading army. The resources of the duchy of Normandy were not equal to the scale of the task, and Duke William was obliged to persuade men from elsewhere in Northern France to join his colours. It helped to have those colours provided by Pope Alexander. According to William of Poitiers, it was not a Norman but an Aquitainian, Aimeri, *vicomte* of Thouars, who spoke first in the debate which followed the submission of London, and urged the duke to become king. William of Poitiers says that all the duke's followers thought him 'outstandingly suitable', but also concedes that they 'wished their gains and honours to be increased by his elevation'. The duke's suitability rested on his 'just cause', the justice of which had been endorsed by no less an authority than the pope. Thereby his co-conquerors could expect rich rewards, without incurring eternal punishment. But the example of the Flemish chroniclers suggests that if papal endorsement did indeed aid recruitment in this way, then its propaganda value was nevertheless short lived.

Duke William and Lanfranc sought the sanction of St Peter's vicar primarily because there could be no higher authority on earth. Their diplomatic initiative was an act of cynical piety. The papal banner which William could flourish sanctified the whole enterprise, however tendentious the grounds on which the pope had been persuaded to grant it. Moreover, according to Orderic, its 'merits' would protect the duke from every danger. The papal sanction could scarcely be gainsaid, other than by opponents of the reform papacy such as Wenric of Trier. And as is demonstrated by the Ordinance issued under the aegis of the papal legate, Ermenfrid of Sion, in Normandy in 1067, 'the authority of the high pontiff' had categorized the invasion as a 'public war', which meant, a just war. On that incontestable authority, the tariff of penances which would normally have been due for sins committed by the invading forces could be reduced, if not entirely remitted. Pope Alexander did not proclaim the Conquest a holy war. No spiritual rewards were offered to participants. But provided the conquerors had fought out of duty to Duke William, and with the right motives, then the holder of St Peter's keys had the authority to let them off some of the penalties which would otherwise have been due for the violence they had inflicted on the English. While unavoidably sinful, such acts of violence in support of a 'just cause' were necessary, even pious. And who, other than the participants themselves, could assess the motives for which they had fought? William of Poitiers conceded as an afterthought that some had hopes of enrichment, but emphasized that they could all nevertheless trust in the justice of the duke's cause.

Thus papal endorsement could offer uniquely advantageous terms to those in search of gain. It was much more than a handy propaganda tool: it got them at least partly off the hook. It had had practical consequences long before papal legates (including the experienced Ermenfrid) arrived in England in 1070 to preside over an extensive purge of the English hierarchy (including, belatedly, Stigand) and their replacement by imported clerics, a wholesale reform of the English church, and (according to Orderic) a 'solemn crowning' of King William in Winchester Cathedral at Easter by the legates themselves. Pope Alexander got far more out of the Conquest than the tyrant Harold's banner, which, according to William of Poitiers, the new king had remitted to him 'as an equal return for the gift sent to him by apostolic generosity'. But it was not a piece of tat: according to William of Poitiers, it depicted an armed warrior worked in the purest gold.

Without the carefully elaborated claim, this papal involvement in the Conquest and its aftermath would not have been possible. But if the desire for papal approval was the principal reason for the claim's initial elaboration, when the Conquest was as yet no more than a glint in the duke's eye, that claim began to exercise a far more profound and pervasive influence as it was successfully asserted. Indeed, it would not be an exaggeration to say that it shaped the way in which the Conquest was implemented.

Implementing William's claim

The first indication that this would be the case followed immediately on the coronation of Christmas Day 1066, which Ermenfrid of Sion's Penitential Ordinance subsequently deemed to have concluded the period of 'public war' by making William king. According to William of Poitiers,

> At London, after his coronation, he made many prudent, just, and merciful provisions; some were for the interest and dignity of that city, others to the profit of the whole race, and not a few to the advantage of the churches of the land.

There is a very striking contrast between this picture of a judicious start to the practice of ruling, and the mayhem which had accompanied the ceremonial inception of the reign, immediately before. Even William of Poitiers had admitted that the inhabitants of London had suffered arson, plunder, and murder at the hands of the French troops during the coronation—from which point, as Ermenfrid would ordain on the pope's behalf in 1067, those troops could no longer benefit from the pope's ameliorated penances.

46

But now those same inhabitants were to benefit from the new king's legislative benevolence.

William of Poitiers' account is corroborated by a sealed writ in Old English proclaiming the king's concession of various privileges to the inhabitants of London. Uniquely for the Conqueror's legislation—indeed, uniquely for early medieval legislation *tout court*—the original document survives. The writ does not, however, purport to establish anything new. Rather, the king

4. William the Conqueror's writ to the Londoners, the only piece of legislation from this period to survive in the original. Even the seal still exists, although it has become detached. Regenbald, Edward the Confessor's 'chancellor' and initially William's, must have been responsible for the writ; it may even be in his hand

announced that he had confirmed to the citizens of London their existing privileges: 'you shall be worthy of all those laws that yet were in King Edward's day'. Paradoxically, his draftsman thereby foreshadowed two new technical terms: what would become 'the law of King Edward', and what would become 'the time of King Edward'. In their mature forms, these neologisms were to play fundamental and enduring roles in demonstrating continuity between Edward the Confessor and the post-Conquest kings. But they had not done so yet.

Even while stressing that absolutely nothing had changed, the draftsman was obliged implicitly to acknowledge the fact of conquest. This diplomatic innovation, unlike King Edward's 'laws' and King Edward's 'day', assumed its mature form from its inception. It was the distinction he drew between the king's 'French and English' subjects, to whom the writ is addressed. It was, of course, mirrored in William of Poitiers' account of the distinct acclamations by 'English' and 'Normans' at the coronation; but even if William of Poitiers accurately described what had happened on Christmas Day 1066, rather than inventing it, the distinction was first committed to writing in the London writ, issued soon after the coronation. The distinction is also reflected in the seal matrix which, with commendable efficiency, had already been engraved for the new king: whereas Edward the Confessor's had the same image of the king in majesty on both sides, the obverse of William's depicted him as duke of the Normans and the reverse as king of the English. Exceptionally, the seal once attached to this writ survives. All these novel terms—'laws' of King Edward, 'King Edward's day', and 'French and English'—may almost certainly be credited to the existing royal secretariat, rather than to new French recruits, since the writ is traditionally executed, and in the vernacular. King William had already installed a new Norman 'portreeve' for London— one of the addressees of the writ—but he does not appear to have replaced the royal scribes. Perhaps a portreeve, unlike a royal scribe, required no technical accomplishments. The only indication that this scribe's ingenuity may have been taxed by his task is the fact that the script is more compressed and angular than is normal in pre-Conquest writs.

Old English royal documents had often referred to the 'day' of a previous king, sometimes in association with a confirmation of the good law which had been in force at that point. In that sense, William's London writ seemed traditional. Thus, for instance, the sole surviving document in King Harold II's name is a writ which confirms rights and privileges to Bishop Giso of Wells (a former royal scribe, who may have drafted the writ himself) 'as fully and freely as ever he held in King Edward's day in all things'. Edward the Confessor, at his accession, may have taken an oath to maintain the laws of Cnut; he certainly renewed them in 1065, as part of the price for settling a revolt by the Northumbrians. Cnut, shortly after his conquest, had confirmed the laws of the great 10th-century king, Edgar, in order to establish his English *bona fides*. Cnut's law codes do indeed recapitulate much existing English legislation, including Edgar's. This was presumably the law of Cnut which Edward the Confessor had repeatedly pledged himself to maintain. With William's London writ, issued at the very beginning of the reign, all earlier royal legislation was, as it were, re-designated King Edward's law (although Edward, unlike Cnut, had never issued a law code). But we shall see that, in the event, this re-designation turned out to be much more than a recapitulation of Old English law. The 'law of King Edward' was to become something which Edward the Confessor would not have recognized.

The Conqueror may have made similar concessions to other cities, although the writs recording them do not survive. We know, for instance, that eventually, after he had faced down a rebellion in Exeter in 1068, he allowed it the same tax remission as it had enjoyed 'in the time of King Edward'. Exeter's tax privilege was equated with one shared by York, Winchester, and London (though it is not specifically mentioned in the London writ). And William of Poitiers records that prior to the coronation, London had submitted on the same terms as Canterbury. Whether or not all these other cities received writs from the Conqueror, the example of Exeter suggests that, in reaffirming the *status quo* under Edward the Confessor, the London writ had established a template for such grants. That template was not restricted to confirmations of the privileges of certain cities. It soon came to set the term of reference for royal confirmations and fresh grants of all kinds.

But it did not do so immediately. A vernacular writ of William recorded that he had granted certain estates to 'Regenbald, my priest...as fully as they were in the hands of King Harold'. It was probably issued before April 1067, and it is highly unusual in referring to Harold as king. Another early vernacular writ confirms all Regenbald's lands as he had held them 'under Edward my kinsman'. The discrepancy suggests that the royal writing office had not yet determined a single point in the past by reference to which tenure should be defined. Yet Regenbald was almost certainly the Conqueror's first 'chancellor'—that is, head of his writing office—as he had been the Confessor's last (and therefore, though this is nowhere recorded, Harold's). King's priests were scribes in his writing office. Although Regenbald, as chancellor, must have been responsible, either directly or ultimately, for the London writ's invocation of 'King Edward's day', he had not yet been forced to work out its implications in the wake of the Conquest. We can be confident that he took particular professional care to get it right where his own interests were concerned.

It would hardly be surprising if a former senior official of King Harold continued, at least in the short term, to refer to him as such; nor that the only other royal document of William's reign to describe Harold as king, dating from 1068, should be a traditional-style Old English diploma in favour of another former member of the royal writing office, Giso, bishop of Wells from 1061. It may have been drafted by Giso

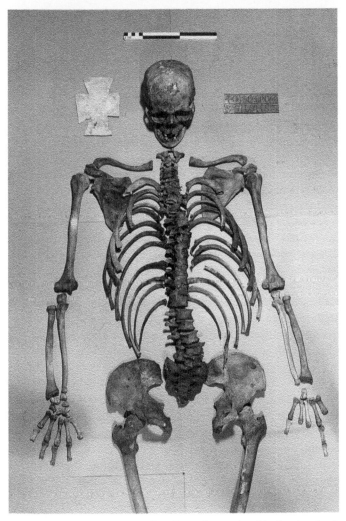

5. The bones of Giso, bishop of Wells, and sometime king's priest (and scribe), with mortuary cross and lead name-plate. It seems that priests in the royal chapel dined well

himself. If it is the last royal document of William's reign to attribute the royal title to Harold, it nevertheless takes care to denigrate him. It is striking that the only surviving royal document in Harold's name is also in favour of Giso, and may also have been drafted by him. For reasons which will become apparent, very soon after the Conquest documents in Harold's name became not simply useless, but positively dangerous. Prudent landholders must have shredded them with embarrassed alacrity. In this respect, Giso seems to have been unusually slow in getting 'on message'. His tardiness does not suggest that he was recalcitrant, or already in his dotage. Rather, it may have arisen because he had persuaded Harold as king to restore certain disputed estates to Wells, and was very anxious to ensure that these restorations were explicitly confirmed by the Conqueror, regardless of the diplomatic niceties. Perhaps he exploited the licence afforded to him by his position as draftsman. We know that, in 1065, he had drafted a diploma of Edward the Confessor in favour of the church of Wells, which was professedly designed to replace earlier royal diplomas 'almost consumed with age'. By 1068, King Harold's treasured writ could hardly have decayed with age, but Giso was determined that the gains it recorded should not share in the oblivion which was already rapidly enveloping Harold. Unlike Regenbald, who retired from royal service in 1067 after overseeing the transition to Norman rule, Giso therefore had a very particular interest in failing to internalize the logic of the new jargon which Regenbald had foreshadowed in the London writ. A bishop who had been importunate enough to secure a letter from Pope Nicholas II, confirming the rights of his see, might even have been prepared to be pushy with the Conqueror.

A third early vernacular writ recorded the Conqueror's grant of lands at Battersea and Pyrford, this time to Westminster Abbey, 'as fully as Harold had it in all things on the day when he was alive and dead'. Harold was not given a royal style here, but another diplomatic neologism—'the day when he was alive and dead'—appears for the first time. The date invoked was of course 14 October, the day of the battle of Hastings. What King Harold had held—the term used in Regenbald's writ—might mean what Harold had held on the day of his death, although the precision of the Westminster writ is novel. Definition of tenure by reference to any point in Harold's reign is, however, clearly incompatible with invocation of the *status quo* 'under Edward my kinsman'.

With the exception of Giso of Wells' 1068 diploma, all of these documents appear to date from the first year of William's reign. Other early writs confirm that initially there was no official line on the point by reference to which tenurial rights were to be defined. Perhaps because the original Westminster writ was later considered to be deficient in this respect—which had become crucial—two variant 12th-century Latin versions of it substitute 'as Earl Harold held...on the day when King Edward was alive and dead'. (There was of course no pressing need to produce improved versions of the writs in favour of Regenbald, who had not been elevated to the episcopal bench on his retirement from the chancellorship.) They show that the neologism 'alive and dead' did not continue to be applied to Harold, but had instead come to be applied to Edward the Confessor. When these spruced-up versions were devised, this had evidently become formulaic. It had been so for a long time. It is evident, for instance, in the corresponding entries in Domesday Book, a massive, comprehensive survey of the whole kingdom, compiled at King William's behest in 1086, which recorded who held what of him.

Domesday: the Survey and the Book

Thus in Domesday Book the land which King William granted to Regenbald is no longer, as in the original writ, said to have been formerly held by 'King Harold'. Rather, 'two thegns held them as two manors in the time of King Edward. Earl Harold joined

6. Even Homer nods: the Domesday scribe's concentration lapsed as he copied out this part of the survey of the king's land in Hampshire. Twice on one folio, he let slip that Harold had been king (though a usurping one). Elsewhere throughout Domesday Book, Harold is consistently entitled 'earl'

them into one.' Of course, if Harold had somehow acquired and combined the estates after Edward's time, then he must have done so as king, as the original writ stated. He had, it will be recalled, become king on the day after Edward's death. But Domesday Book is very particular both about recording who held 'in the time of King Edward'—*tempore regis Edwardi* or 'T.R.E.', as the Domesday acronym has it—and implausibly specifying that Harold had been an earl when he had held and conjoined the two estates. Even the title earl is a grudging interlinear insertion. Again, those estates which King William confirmed to Regenbald—which Regenbald was said in the original writ to have held 'under my kinsman Edward'—are in Domesday Book recorded formulaically as having been held by Regenbald 'T.R.E.'. Finally, the Domesday entries corresponding to the Westminster writ do not say explicitly that Harold had held Battersea and Pyrford *T.R.E.*, but that he held Battersea as earl, and Pyrford 'of King Edward'. In other words, Domesday Book is quite clearly recording what it claims was the situation *T.R.E.*, without in these instances using the acronym. In the case of the fresh grant to Regenbald, Domesday was forced, perhaps by the terms of the original writ, to draw a veil over the fact that the estates had first been held by Harold as king. In the case of Battersea and Pyrford, there was no need to make any allusion, however closet, to the period of Harold's reign.

Papal intervention

Stalwart efforts were made to avoid such allusions. When this proved impossible, a circumlocution would be devised in this otherwise most terse of records: 'These five lands were taken by Earl Harold after the death of King Edward'; or 'after the death of King Edward . . . before King William came'. It is a remarkable testimony to the powers of concentration of the Domesday scribe that there were only two occasions when he nodded, by referring to 'when Harold usurped the kingdom', and 'when he was reigning'. These quite exceptional slips serve to highlight the chronological framework of Domesday Book, explicitly stated in the surviving questionnaire for the inquest, the findings of which are engrossed in the Book. All the questions had to be answered with respect to three points in time: now, that is, 1086; when the land was given, a point which varied from case to case, and which, probably for that reason, was often fudged or omitted; and *T.R.E.* 1086 and *T.R.E.* are present, either explicitly or implicitly, in almost every entry. It is of course from Domesday Book that we know that Exeter had enjoyed the same tax remission as Winchester, York, and London 'T.R.E.'. And it can be demonstrated from a preliminary draft for the southwestern shires known as the *Liber Exoniensis*, which was further condensed in Domesday Book itself, that *T.R.E.* is not simply a general reference to Edward the Confessor's reign. Rather, it meant 'the day on which King Edward was alive and dead'. The phrase which had first appeared with respect to Harold in the Conqueror's early vernacular writ in favour of Westminster Abbey, had been reapplied to Edward the Confessor. In that form it was intrinsic to Domesday Book.

That it had become so is not evidence of an intense historical curiosity on the part of the man who devised the inquest, and whose (largely) un-nodding scribe engrossed the Book. William of St Calais, bishop of Durham, like Lanfranc, was an adroit lawyer and administrator imported from Normandy, not an historian. By the time Bishop William planned the inquest, the comprehensive, systematic recording of the *status quo T.R.E.* had assumed paramount importance. It had done so because the London writ's (traditional-style) 'day of King Edward' had been transformed into the (novel) 'day on which King Edward had been alive and dead'. Harold II's sole surviving writ had confirmed lands as they had been held in King Edward's day, because he was being presented as Edward's successor. The Conqueror's London writ confirmed the customs of King Edward's day, because he, too, was being presented as Edward's successor, not Harold's. Implicit in the premises of the London writ was a refusal to acknowledge that anything which had been obtained under Harold could be legitimate. It was no great conceptual leap to deny that Harold had ever been king. William of Poitiers, as we have seen, did not quite make that leap. Like the author of the captions to the Bayeux Tapestry, he still called Harold king, though a fatally perjured one. As the author of an historical narrative, albeit one replete with tendentious and invented material, he, like William of Jumièges before him, could not simply airbrush Harold's reign from history. Nevertheless, they both recapitulated the claim which Gilbert fitzOsbern had presented to the papal curia in 1066. That claim would come to necessitate such an airbrushing, at least in legal terms, once title to land was defined by reference to the last point of legitimacy prior to William's accession as king. If Domesday Book were quarried as a source of historical fact, it would require a very alert and suspicious reader to infer that 'Earl Harold' had ever been king, or that England had been conquered by the duke of Normandy. Of course, the Book purported to be an objective record of such facts. But because by its very nature it lacked a narrative structure, it could suppress inconvenient facts and, where unavoidable, invent convenient ones, in an even more blatantly tendentious way than William of Jumièges and William of Poitiers.

The Conqueror's earliest writs reveal that this was not true of official documents from the very start. There was, as we have seen, a brief period of indecision and experiment. But from a year or so after his coronation, his vernacular writs begin consistently to use the phrase coined in the London writ. His Latin writs and diplomas start to refer to *tempore regis Edwardi*, and variants thereof. In other words, the template of the London writ, which was traditional, in conjunction with the king's claim, which was novel, had already laid down the baseline which would be intrinsic to the Domesday inquest. It was fundamental to the inquest because it had become formulaic by 1086. The legal baseline had been fixed by the interplay between conflicting claims to land throughout the reign. The premises that (1) William was Edward's legitimately designated successor, having been granted the kingdom by him as a *post obitum* gift; and (2) that Harold was a tyrannical usurper who had never legitimately been king, had been pushed to their logical conclusion.

The application of this principle may be seen clearly in many of the records of royal adjudication of disputed claims in which churches were involved during the 1070s and 1080s. Thus, in the early 1070s, the abbot of Ely succeeded in recovering land which was found to have been in the abbey's demesne 'in the time of King Edward'—and associated documents reveal that this was synonymous with 'the day on which King Edward was alive and dead'. The mature procedure is well illustrated by a writ of 1082, summoning a court to try yet again to settle the disputes relating to Ely's estates. The king commanded that

> many of those Englishmen should be chosen who know how the lands of the aforesaid church lay on the day when King Edward died, and let them confirm what they say by oath. When this has been done, let the lands of the church be restored which were in its demesne on the day of Edward's death, except for those which men claim that I have given them...

Inquest procedure was used to elicit English testimony as to the *status quo* at the defining point. In that respect, this writ foreshadows procedure in the Domesday inquest. But even in the case of a church—a landholder which, unlike the vast majority of wealthy laymen, had survived the Conquest—this would not result in a blanket restoration of that *status quo*. The king was not in that sense bound by it. A gift from him could trump it, if he so wished. But as the Conqueror's few surviving writs demonstrate (testimony recorded in Domesday suggests that there were once hundreds, if not thousands), precisely what he gave to whomever he chose was defined in terms of that *status quo*. Indeed, the king's primacy is implicit in the *status quo*: the day of Edward the Confessor's death had become definitive in this way solely because of its significance in William's claim to the kingdom. There was nothing analogous in pre-Conquest English (or for that matter Norman) documentation. Though the rights given were defined by reference to the *status quo*, the fact that the decision as to who would hold lay with the king alone transformed the rights held. They now depended solely on the king.

The terms in which those rights were described remained largely unchanged, although very soon writs began to be issued in duplicate, with Latin translations for the new audience of Francophone settlers, and ultimately, it seems, the substitution of Latin for Old English. The very process of translation, in which familiar English words were rendered by unfamiliar Norman Latin ones, involved distortion, which reflected a change in the meaning of those rights. Translation perforce involves interpretation. This is very obvious in Domesday Book, for which there appears never to have been any Old English parallel text. William of St Calais, or some other official, had clearly devised an official glossary for the translation of the English testimony on which the Book was based. That glossary included many Latin terms unknown in pre-Conquest England. The surviving Englishmen who testified would have had increasing difficulty recognizing the rights which were defined by reference to the *status quo* on the day of Edward's death.

One Domesday term for which there was no known English equivalent is *antecessor*. In canon law this meant a predecessor in ecclesiastical office. In this sense it is used in Lanfranc's canon law collection. But in Domesday Book, and earlier writs and diplomas of the Conqueror, an *antecessor* was the person who was deemed to have held at the crucial point, *T.R.E.*, 5 January 1066. In this very particular sense, secular landholders had *antecessores* in the same way as ecclesiastical ones. The estates of churches, however, tended to be much the same after the Conquest as before, despite the impression given by the surviving land pleas, in which a great deal of fuss was made about small scale losses. By contrast, Domesday Book itself betrays that the pattern of secular landholding was completely shredded. In the case of churches, all the lands and rights deemed to have been held by one *antecessor* were held by a single successor. Indeed, in a very few exceptional cases—for instance, Wulfstan, bishop of Worcester, his rival Æthelwig, abbot of Evesham, and, of course, Giso of Wells—sitting pre-Conquest prelates who proved themselves indispensable to the Conqueror might be exempted from the otherwise widespread purge of the English hierarchy, initiated under the aegis of the papal legates in 1070. A few exceptional clerical *antecessores*, in other words, were allowed to survive, and to prosper. With laymen, by contrast, there was no simple pattern of a single individual succeeding to all the lands and rights of single *antecessor*, still less of *antecessores* being allowed to survive. Nor did one Frenchman necessarily succeed to all the lands and rights of a number of *antecessores*. Rather, the estates with which the Conqueror rewarded those who had fought for him were spatchcocked together from parcels which consisted of some, but not necessarily all, of what any number of individuals were deemed to have held severally *T.R.E.* Where laymen were concerned, the *antecessor* was a device for defining precisely the rights of a new tenant in a particular parcel of land, which in most cases constituted only a part of his estate. But although it was—or purported to be—precise in a chronological sense, it was demonstrably not always so in other senses. Thus, for instance, what an *antecessor* was deemed to have held in some instances excluded, and in others included, what was said to have been held by men commended to the *antecessor* as their lord. In other words, the blanket term 'held' might be interpreted in different ways from case to case, and could cover a multitude of sins. Its potential ambiguity created the scope for vigorous disputation, later on, of rights claimed to derive from an *antecessor*, or 'through inheritance of his *antecessor*', as one Domesday entry revealingly puts it, perhaps reproducing the words of the witnesses. Moreover, the possible confusion was compounded by the fact that several Domesday tenants might share an *antecessor* because they had each succeeded to different rights held by that *antecessor*. Ambiguities of these and other kinds explain many of the disputes recorded in the land pleas of the 1070s and 1080s, and more plentifully, if more tersely, in Domesday Book itself.

The *antecessor*, defined by his tenure at the death of Edward the Confessor, was thus a rough and ready means for administering the wholesale redistribution of land in conquered England. It imposed a principle of a sort, and avoided the danger of anarchic land-grabbing, even if in its practical simplicity it failed to resolve every conceivable ambiguity.

The very term indicated its origin, for it was, or became, axiomatic that Edward the Confessor, not Harold, was the Conqueror's *antecessor*, just as Robert of Jumièges, not Stigand, was Lanfranc's. That axiom had been formulated even before Lanfranc became archbishop of Canterbury in 1070. This is suggested not only by the claim which Gilbert, archdeacon of Lisieux rehearsed before the papal curia early in 1066, but also by two very similar royal diplomas which were almost certainly issued on the same splendid occasion: Matilda's consecration as queen by Ealdred of York, in Westminster Abbey on 11 May 1068. Both these documents describe Edward as William's *antecessor*. One of them confirmed the endowment and privileges of the church of St Martin's-le-Grand, London, for William's priest Ingelric, its dean, who may previously have served Edward in a similar capacity. The other is the Wells diploma with which we are already very familiar. It may therefore not be fanciful to attribute the coining of this term, like 'King Edward's day', 'King Edward's laws', and 'alive and dead', to old chancery hands, and perhaps in this instance to Giso himself. It is unclear who drafted the St Martin's diploma, but almost certain that Giso was responsible for the stylistically similar Wells one. Yet if Giso (or alternatively Ingelric) first coined *antecessor* in a diplomatic context, he did so in order to encapsulate the fundamental premises of King William's claim to the throne, which had already been devised by others.

The description of Edward as William's *antecessor* in Giso's diploma obviously did not imply a *damnatio memoriae* for King Harold, because the diploma explicitly confirmed Harold's restoration of lands to Wells. But as we have seen, the diploma was, in its treatment of Harold, exceptional. Thereafter that implication of the Conqueror's claim was rapidly realized in the documentation of the reign. In Domesday Book, Edward is never termed William's *antecessor*, or William his successor, perhaps because they are always referred to by title and, often, by name. But by then the term, coined for Edward the Confessor, had come to be applied instead to the person deemed to have held the specified piece of land on the day when Edward, the model for all *antecessores*, had last held the kingdom.

It tended to be used explicitly in Domesday only when it was necessary to spell out some current claim, because of an unresolved dispute. Parchment was valuable, and not to be wasted on otiose verbosity. But every appearance of the acronym 'T.R.E.', in almost every entry in Domesday, is implicitly the invocation of rights supposedly derived from one or more *antecessores*. Like the king's claim, the term was intended to demonstrate continuity with Edwardian England. Every landholder had succeeded to one or more *antecessores*, just as the king had succeeded to his *antecessor*. This is one reason why even a careful reader of Domesday Book might form the impression that nothing much had changed in England since the time of King Edward. Yet it is Domesday Book which can be made to reveal that the tenurial patterns of Edwardian England, particularly with respect to laymen, had been shredded, even as those lands were granted out according to what were established by English testimony to have been the rights of Edwardian tenants. Paradoxically, Domesday Book is our best source for undermining the demonstration of continuity, for which it is also our most extensive and detailed source. That fictive continuity was a systematic misrepresentation of the English past. It sprang from the misrepresentation of the events of Edward's reign in which the Conqueror's claim was grounded, the most detailed extant summary of which is preserved by William of Poitiers.

Indeed, one might go even further. It was the way in which William of St Calais' commissioners attempted to demonstrate continuity with Edwardian England which inadvertently revealed how continuity had been severed. For the concept of the *antecessor* reads back into the Old English past a dependency on the king which was quite foreign to it. It assumes that a strictly dependent system of tenurial lordship which, as we shall see, Domesday shows had been imposed on England by 1086, already existed under Edward the Confessor. Yet much of the English testimony preserved in Domesday Book confirms what is suggested by other sources: that in pre-Conquest England one did not necessarily hold one's land of one's lord; that many Edwardian landholders could, as another Domesday formula puts it, go to any lord they chose with their land; and that if one did hold land from a lord, on a lease, one might also have a different, purely personal, lord. If the relationship between lord and man in pre-Conquest England had no necessary connection with the tenure of land, then it follows that the king could not have been the source of all legitimate tenure in England in the time of King Edward. Yet that is one way of putting the assumption on which the Domesday *antecessor* is based. It was William's claim that he alone was Edward's chosen successor, that Edward had bequeathed the kingdom to him, that made England his and his alone. It was on that basis that the king became the source of all tenure. Edward the Confessor might have been the lord of all, but they had not all held their lands, directly or intermediately, of him.

The tenurial dependence on the king which is implicitly, and erroneously, imposed upon Old England by the Domesday *antecessor* is intrinsic to the very layout of the Book. Initially it is divided into shires, Old English administrative and judicial units of some antiquity. The survey of each shire begins with the *terra Regis*—the land exploited on the king's behalf by his agents, rather than granted out—followed by the lands held immediately of him by his *tenentes in capite* ('tenants in head'), or tenants-in-chief, as this phrase is conventionally translated. A preliminary, numbered list of tenants-in-chief could be used rapidly to identify the corresponding, numbered entry for each tenant-in-chief within the shire. The lands which tenants-in-chief had in turn granted out to their men were not recorded on a tenurial basis. They were organized by hundred—the Old English administrative and judicial units of which shires were constituted—because a jury from each hundred testified to the accuracy of responses to the inquest's questions, and the testimony of these hundredal juries, half English and half French, was recorded by stenographers in the meetings of the shire court where the information was collected. This feature makes it quite clear that the primary concern of Domesday Book was with the tenants-in-chief; it had little interest in those subtenants on whose testimony it was nevertheless built. Not one of the jurors who can be identified from other sources is even mentioned by name in Domesday. The focus on tenants-in-chief also demonstrates the reality of the tenurial dependence which had been imposed on England by the Conquest. The Book was designed to be used by royal administrators, and they were primarily interested in those who held immediately of the king. Comparatively seldom does the Book record the king's grant of the particular piece of land, the second—and by definition the only variable—point is time specified in the terms of reference of the inquest. As with explicit identifications of *antecessores*, to do so would have been needlessly repetitive, and William of St Calais was consummately concise. In the cases of both the *antecessor* and tenurial dependence on the king, the point was identical, and too fundamental to need spelling out, except in rare unresolved disputes.

By the time Domesday Book was compiled, there were only a handful of English lay tenants-in-chief left who were recorded as having also held before the Conquest, and they held only small estates. Most of these exceptions were royal servants or officials, who were presumably kept on to serve the new regime. There were of course more surviving prelates, who were categorized as tenants-in-chief in Domesday. For as the preliminary directories in each shire make clear, bishops and most abbots were considered to hold the lands of their churches immediately of the king, on much the same terms as lay tenants-in-chief. Of those existing prelates who survived the purges of the English hierarchy, William, bishop of London (one of the addressees of the London writ) died in 1075 and Æthelwig of Evesham in 1078, but Giso of Wells lived until 1088, and Wulfstan of Worcester until 1094.

In the immediate aftermath of the Conquest, however, the survival rate for laymen as well as clerics was initially higher. Many had died in the pitched battles of 1066 and the subsequent rearguard actions, others had fled into exile. Their lands were likely to be forfeit, and allocated to others. But those Englishmen who did not fit into these categories—who demonstrably included some laymen and (until the arrival of the papal legates in 1070) most prelates—were, in the words of the worldly wise Peterborough chronicler, allowed to 'buy back their lands' from the new king; or as William of Poitiers put it, the Conqueror 'restored to them everything which they had possessed' in return for their oaths. Domesday Book occasionally refers in passing to this process, by which 'the English redeemed their lands'. In Suffolk, it seems, it was administered by none other than Ingelric, the king's priest who solicited the 1068 diploma in favour of St Martin's-le-Grand; in Hampshire by William fitzOsbern, builder of Winchester Castle and father of Gilbert fitzOsbern, the ducal ambassador at the papal curia in 1066. Domesday Book does not specify when they administered this redemption, but William fitzOsbern died in 1071, so it must have been very early in the reign.

In other words, it was not only new French tenants who held, in William of Poitiers' words, 'rich benefices' as grantees of the king. We know that at least some of those Englishmen who were permitted to survive, both lay and clerical, were forced not only to acknowledge that they now held their lands on a new basis, of the king, but to pay him for the privilege. Brand, abbot of Peterborough, had to pay through the nose because, as the Peterborough chronicler laments, he had, soon after the battle of Hastings, made the catastrophic error of seeking Edgar *ætheling*'s assent to his election as abbot, under the impression that Edgar 'would be king'. The lands which King William confirmed included estates given to the abbey after Edward the Confessor's death and prior to William's coronation, so William was clearly prepared to fudge, if the price was right. It is striking that both Ingelric the priest and William fitzOsbern are amongst the witnesses of the royal diploma which sealed this deal. Even at this very early stage in the new reign, they seem already to have been in training for their role in the redemption of land by the English.

Unlike surviving Englishmen, new French tenants-in-chief did not have to 'redeem' their lands from the Conqueror. But in those exceptional cases when Domesday Book was obliged to describe the king's grants to them, the conveyance seems to have been effected in the same way as to the few surviving Englishmen. A sealed writ was sent to the sheriff of the relevant shire, instructing him to ensure that the royal grant was implemented. We may infer that such writs were, at least for the time being, sent in duplicate, in English and Latin, and read out in the shire (or sometimes the hundred) court, because Domesday Book often records the testimony of hundredal jurors that they had heard (or not heard) the king's writ, or in one case his seal (for the royal seal was much more noticeable to a lay audience than the attached scrap of parchment which it authenticated), 'or the *liberator* who seised him with it'. Where the *liberator* is identifiable, he is the sheriff. The term is never used in this sense in pre-Conquest documents, and there appears to be no Old English equivalent. Indeed, it is revealing that Domesday Book never refers to *liberatores T.R.E.* In this particular sense, Domesday implicitly acknowledges, the term is a post-Conquest neologism. In other contexts it most commonly signified Christ, as redeemer or deliverer of fallen man. On Lanfranc's instructions, William the Conqueror allegedly had his jester flogged as a blasphemer for exclaiming at the sight of his crowned master: 'Behold, I see God!'

Lanfranc may have thought such a comparison sacrilegious, even when made in jest. But whoever coined the term *liberator* for the king's agents must have had the same analogy in mind, at least with respect to the king's powers over the tenure of land. Its etymology suggests its Domesday meaning: all land in conquered England which was not held by the king himself, as Edward the Confessor's successor, was in a sense redeemed from—or freed by—the king. In other words, conquering Frenchmen and surviving Englishmen both held land solely by grace of the king.

The uniqueness of the king's role is suggested by the fact that only he had agents termed *liberatores*. In those unusual cases where we know that he had intervened to secure the grant of a subtenancy, the *liberator* was his, not the new beneficiary's lord's. The king's *liberatores* are recorded as having 'seised' tenants: in one shire the term *saisitor* is used as a synonym for *liberator*. It is also noteworthy that *saisire*, for which there is no obvious Old English translation, appears in no genuine pre-Conquest Latin document. Its etymology is evidently French, from *saisir*, to grasp. It is, in other words, another Norman neologism. In Domesday and in the Conqueror's writs it means 'to give into the grasp of'.

There is no indication of what a *liberator* did in order to effect this apparently new form of conveyance on the king's behalf, other than, we may conjecture, to deliver the writ to or perhaps to read it out in the appropriate forum. But in a few, exceptional cases we do have a record of the king making a grant in person, even very occasionally in Domesday Book. The most revealing of these is, however, an account in a diploma, probably issued at Easter 1069 'in the royal town which in the English tongue is called Guerith [Winchester]'. Diplomas are more discursive than writs, as is suggested by the help this one affords to a Norman audience. On occasion, they are therefore more revealing. This diploma recorded that the king had given, at William fitzOsbern's suggestion, 'the land which in English is called Harmondsworth' to the abbey of La Trinité-du-Mont, Rouen. Simple logistics made it impossible for the king to lay an object, such as a knife, on the altar of the abbey, which was a customary way of symbolizing a donation to a church. Instead, as was also quite common, the king made as if to give a knife to the abbot, who was in attendance on him. But rather than simply handing it to Abbot Rainier, William, 'in jocular fashion', pretended that he was going to stab it through the abbot's grasping palm. 'That's the way land ought to be given!', he is said to have jested to the startled courtiers standing around. This incident reveals how 'seising' a new tenant might be symbolically effected. It also, quite exceptionally, makes a jest of the violence of the Conquest, which, as we have seen, was usually masked in elaborate legal formality. What had been taken violently could—in this case, according to the king himself, should—be granted out violently, and by the king alone. According to William of Poitiers and the Bayeux Tapestry, at a critical juncture during the battle of Hastings William had raised his helmet, like some latter day classical hero, to show his face to his panicking troops. Thereby the duke reassured them that there was no truth in the rumour that he had been killed, and restored their morale. On this occasion in 1069, the king seems, quite exceptionally, to have deliberately let slip the mask of propriety which had partially concealed the Conquest from its inception.

However violent the practice might be, that legalistic propriety insinuated itself into Norman attitudes. At William's funeral, held in his foundation of St-Étienne, Caen, where Lanfranc had been the first abbot, the officiating prelate, the bishop of Evreux, asked the congregation to forgive their dead lord any wrongs he had committed against them. This provoked an outraged expression of grievance from a certain Ascelin, who asserted, according to Orderic Vitalis, that William had built the abbey church on land which he had 'violently stolen' from Ascelin's father. Ascelin now laid claim to it, 'forbidding in God's name that the body of this robber be covered with earth that is mine or buried in my inheritance'. That Ascelin did not act until the Conqueror was dead suggests that even a barrack room lawyer

7. St-Étienne, Caen: William's foundation, and the setting for his funeral. Notoriously, proceedings were interrupted by a certain Ascelin, who demanded compensation for the land which William had appropriated from Ascelin's father in order to build the church

would be prudent about invoking such proprieties against the king in person. It was much less perilous to take on his corpse. But that, in these dramatic circumstances, he was successful in delaying William's interment until he had received satisfaction suggests that the overwhelming force of hereditary claims was universally acknowledged. The bishop of Evreux's funeral sermon had, again according to Orderic, emphasized how William had 'valiantly extended the frontiers where Norman law prevails; how, more than all his *antecessores*, he had elevated his race'. What is noteworthy is not that William's ducal predecessors, rather than his royal ones, should here be described as his *antecessores*. This was quite common in Norman sources. Rather, it is remarkable that the bishop of Evreux was none other than Gilbert fitzOsbern, sometime archdeacon of Lisieux and ambassador to the papal curia in 1066. No-one, we may presume, had a better grasp of the dodgy nature of the duke's dossier. Ascelin's unexpected response to Gilbert's sanctimonious plea to the congregation for forgiveness must have prompted the bishop to reflect anew on the sanctity of hereditary claims. The irony was that they had become all the more incontestable because of the success with which William had contested the tendentious claim which Gilbert had expounded in Rome in 1066. And in conquered England, unlike Normandy, no heirs succeeded to estates other than by the king's favour. Only thus could anyone become a tenant, in Domesday's words, 'through inheritance of his *antecessor*'. Gilbert's father, William fitzOsbern, had been one of those officials charged with ensuring that surviving Englishmen were also forced to acknowledge this fundamental fact.

William the Conqueror's role as the source of all tenure in conquered England was unique and unprecedented. It sprang from his claim that he, and he alone, was Edward the Confessor's successor. That claim, as we have seen, provided the framework for Domesday Book. Legalistic precision, brutal practicality, and the rewriting of history went hand in hand. The claim shaped the way in which land was redistributed in conquered England.

In doing so, it created a logical conundrum for which there was no solution, and which was to have profound consequences for the rest of English history. The unacknowledged difference between the king's relationship with his *antecessor*, Edward, and his men's relationship with theirs, was that his arose solely from Edward's bequest, whereas theirs, as we have also seen, was created by William's grant. They depended on him, but he depended on no-one. This discrepancy was intrinsic to the system of dependent tenure which William's claim had created in England. It meant that the position in which the king's immediate tenants found themselves was precarious in the extreme. Although that precariousness was ameliorated in the 12th century, the logic of dependency continued to be the dominant fact in English political history for centuries, and determined many of the unique characteristics of medieval England. It is, therefore, necessary to probe in a little more detail the evidence for the imposition of dependency in the early years after the Conquest. Unsurprisingly, much of this is ecclesiastical.

Chapter 3
The bonds of tenure, ecclesiastical and secular

In invoking Eadmer of Canterbury as a uniquely perceptive analyst of what he termed the 'strange changes' and 'developments which were quite unknown in former days' which followed the Conquest, we are in the best of scholarly company. For William of Malmesbury said of Eadmer that 'He describes everything so clearly that it all seems to happen before our very eyes.' In his *History of Novelties*, Eadmer said that he would confine himself to ecclesiastical affairs, omitting any innovations which the Conqueror had made in the secular sphere. Nevertheless, he adds with a heavy hint to his reader, 'from what he ordained in divine matters...the character [of such secular innovations] may be inferred'. The 'seed' of all these changes, both ecclesiastical and secular, is identified in the book's preface:

> From the time that William, count of Normandy, subdued this land to himself by war, no-one...was made a bishop or abbot in it who had not first been made the king's man (*homo*), and had received investiture of his bishopric or abbacy from the king's hand...

Eadmer thought that this sacrilegious practice, unknown in pre-Conquest England, was imported from Normandy; but he was as mistaken in this as he was in his view that everything had depended on the duke's 'nod' in Normandy. The former novelty was a specific, ecclesiastical manifestation of the latter, which was

8. Crozier of Ranulf Flambard, bishop of Durham, and William Rufus'
ruthless administrator of vacant churches

in truth unique to conquered England. In a detailed examination of the appointment of Lanfranc's successor, Anselm, as archbishop of Canterbury, Eadmer demonstrates that a bishop- or abbot-elect entered into office not when he was elected or even consecrated, but when he became the king's man (*homo*). He did so when the king accepted his homage (*homagium*), which meant, when he was allowed to kneel in front of the king and place his hands between the king's. Eadmer rightly considers that it was this ceremony which formally gave him the lands of the church in question, and in doing so made him its prelate. He makes this point very clearly in a detailed account of Anselm's accession as archbishop of Canterbury. Tenure of land and office had become indistinguishable. This was the 'seed' which the Conquest had planted.

Eadmer was not simply indulging in indignant hyperbole. His analysis of the implications of the imposition of dependent tenure on churchmen is an accurate one, as we might expect of a former scribe in the archbishop of Canterbury's writing office. He examines one consequence of this imposition of dependent tenure on prelates in England: on the death of a prelate, the land of his church reverted into the king's hand. The king's agents administered the estates, and took the profits, of vacant churches. A plethora of evidence, including Domesday Book's categorization of prelates as tenants-in-chief, confirms that this was indeed what happened to the lands of churches on the death of a prelate. As Eadmer says, the king's 'nod' affected bishops, abbots and 'other *principes*' in the same way.

This practice of reversion—or usurpation, as Eadmer pointedly termed it—explained why post-Conquest kings often kept churches vacant. It meant that there was a sacrilegious logic to the Conqueror's son and successor as king, William Rufus, claiming to be archbishop after Lanfranc's death and prior to Anselm's appointment. Rufus was minded to exploit these powers ruthlessly, and was ably served in this capacity by Ranulf

9. Ely Cathedral (then Abbey): it is just possible to detect the break in building during the vacancy between 1093 and 1100, when the abbey was in the king's hands. The break runs from the north-east corner of the north transept to the easternmost bay of the south aisle of the nave

Flambard, of 'sharp intellect and ready tongue', as the Durham house historian Symeon described him. Ranulf was subsequently rewarded with the bishopric of Durham (after administering the church for three years during the preceding vacancy). According to some Winchester annals, death seemed preferable to life for tenants on the estates of vacant churches under William Rufus, so ruthless was the royal exploitation. Royal administration during a vacancy was not simply a matter of fleecing the tenants. The rebuilding of the (then) abbey church at Ely seems to have stopped abruptly in 1093, at a highly impractical point, when the abbey reverted into Rufus's hand. We know this because the evidence is still visible. Construction did not recommence until a new abbot was appointed by Rufus's successor, Henry I, on the day of his coronation in 1100. Rufus had been determined to pocket the maximum possible income, and had therefore suspended the current building project as soon as the church reverted into his hand.

It so happens that in the cases of the two exceptional English prelates who survived and prospered under the Conqueror— Wulfstan of Worcester and his rival Æthelwig, abbot of Evesham—there is explicit evidence that on their deaths their churches came into the hands of (respectively) Rufus and his father. In Wulfstan's case, Rufus issued a writ, which announced that 'on the death of the bishop the honour returned into my hand', and exacted payments from sitting tenants on the estates of the church of Worcester. Unsurprisingly, Ranulf Flambard appears at the top of the witness list. In Æthelwig's case, a near contemporary administrative document records that the church of Evesham was then 'under the king's hand' for a while, until a successor was appointed. In other words, Eadmer was wrong to imply that only new bishops and abbots depended on the king as a result of the Conquest. Survivors from the reign of Edward the Confessor did so too, though Eadmer was right to imply that they had not done under Edward. The Conquest had transformed existing prelates as well as new ones into tenants-in-chief, holding precariously of the king. The lands of their churches fell into the king's hand on their deaths, even though the king's predecessor, Edward, had not granted them those lands when they had been appointed.

In turn, this suggests that there had been an ecclesiastical aspect to the redemption of land by the English at the beginning of the Conqueror's reign. Traces of the process survive. In the preliminary draft of Domesday Book for the southwestern circuit, known as the *Liber Exoniensis*, the values of certain manors which Giso, bishop of Wells had already held as bishop on the day of Edward the Confessor's death are also recorded as they were later, 'when he received' them. Giso must have 'received' them from the Conqueror. Perhaps the royal diploma of 1068, discussed in the last chapter, recorded the occasion. The Conqueror probably issued writs of confirmation to every sitting prelate—we have already noticed the case of the maladroit Abbot Brand of Peterborough. This practice seems to have been traditional; but traditional confirmation had assumed a novel significance with William the Conqueror. The most suggestive piece of evidence is a writ sent to Æthelwig of Evesham, probably in 1072 or 1073. It ordered him to bring the five knights he owed 'for your abbey' to the king. This is the first surviving piece of evidence for the duty of tenants-in-chief, including, obviously, ecclesiastical tenants-in-chief, to supply a specific number of knights, on demand, to the king.

Knight service and 'feudalism'

The debate about whether knight service quotas owed by tenants-in-chief to the king were an innovation, a continuation, or an adaptation of the Old English system of military service, based on the hide, has for centuries been central to any assessment of the Conquest. Whether the Conqueror introduced feudalism to England—whether there was continuity or discontinuity—has been deemed to depend on one's answer to this question. Direct evidence from the Conqueror's reign of quotas owed to the king—as opposed to quotas owed by subtenants to their lords—is limited to this writ. But it is possible to establish from returns to a survey of tenants-in-chief carried out in 1166 and from the pipe rolls—the central royal financial accounts which seem to have been initiated in the reign of Henry I—that the quotas were imposed, quickly, artificially, and often quite arbitrarily, from above. The original quotas were always multiples of five, and they bore little relation to the extent of the lands held by the tenants-in-chief who owed them. The arguments based on this late evidence are very technical, but the conclusion is irrefragable. The Evesham writ shows that they must have been imposed at the very latest by 1073. Abbot Æthelwig is responsible not only for his own quota, but for mustering the quotas owed by other landholders over a wide area of the West Midlands for which the king had made him a sort of military governor, the closest analogy to his role being that of an Old English earl. The quotas bore no relation to the Old English hide-based system, which continued to operate in parallel for raising the traditional army, or *fyrd*. They therefore constituted another quick, practical response, like the *murdrum* fine and the construction of castles, to the pressing problems of military occupation. This is suggested by the fact that, like castles, they failed to pay even lip service to the fiction of continuity. That the sitting abbot of Evesham owed a (favourably light) quota shows that this new obligation had been imposed not just on Normans, whether clerical or lay, to whom the king gave lands, but on surviving Edwardian tenants too. That they were owed only by tenants-in-chief shows that they were a function of that immediate dependency on the king which Eadmer had identified as the primary novelty of the Conquest. It is impossible to prove that the Conqueror imposed them either when he first gave the land or (in the case of surviving Englishmen) when the land was redeemed from him; but it is difficult to conceive of a more likely or suitable occasion for his doing so. The quota was one element in a personal deal, struck between the king and a particular individual. Like reversion to the king on the death of a tenant-in-chief, it is a mark of novel post-Conquest dependency. In the case of Æthelwig of Evesham and, by inference, other surviving Edwardian prelates, it constituted one of the terms on which, henceforth, they held the lands of their churches of the king.

Eadmer concentrates on the innovatory precariousness of tenure-in-chief, whether clerical or (he prompts his readers to infer) lay, but he says nothing about knight service quotas. Nor does Domesday Book, although its primary concern is evidently with the lands held by each tenant-in-chief within each shire. The Book was designed to make it a quick, easy matter for royal officials in Winchester Castle, where the Book was kept, to calculate the precise extent and value of such lands, for instance on the death of the tenant, whether lay or clerical, and to instruct relevant sheriffs accordingly. If the land in question had reverted into the king's hand, the sheriff needed to know exactly how much more the royal treasury would expect from him in his annual return. There was no need for the Book to record knight service quotas, which must have been well known to the central royal bureaucracy. That much is clear from the pipe rolls.

Homage, 'the oath of Salisbury', and Domesday

The Book also fails to say anything about the ceremony of homage on which, by contrast, Eadmer lays heavy emphasis. In many respects, it was like a vast diploma: diplomas (or writs) very seldom said anything about the ceremonial form of the grant which they recorded. Moreover, the jurors on whose testimony Domesday Book was based were unlikely to have witnessed the constitutive act of homage; they testified to hearing (or not hearing) the writ which proclaimed, in the shire or hundred court, the tenurial consequence of that act. It is therefore unsurprising that the Book should ignore the ceremony which, according to Eadmer, created the bond between royal lord and ecclesiastical tenant-in-chief. That bond was at once personal and tenurial;

because it was personal, it was severed by the death of a prelate. A new one would be created only by the king's acceptance of the putative successor's *homagium*, a term so recently coined that Eadmer, who had a quick ear for neologisms which one would expect of an amanuensis, began to use it only half way through his book. This, in Eadmer's view, was the Conqueror's principal innovation, the seed from which the peculiar evils of post-Conquest England grew. According to the chronicle of Evesham Abbey, which was not written until the early 13th century, but which is demonstrably based on much earlier sources, Æthelwig's successor became abbot only when William the Conqueror accepted his homage. Was Eadmer right, however, to hint that these evils flourished in the secular sphere too?

The evidence is much thinner and more difficult to evaluate. But in one respect lay tenancies-in-chief, other than those briefly held by a few English survivors, must have been different from ecclesiastical ones. Perhaps in accordance with the Penitential Ordinance's stipulation that penitent invaders who had no idea how many Englishmen they had killed 'should build or enlarge a church', the Conqueror founded Battle Abbey on the site of his victory, its high altar allegedly constructed on the very spot where Harold II's 'standard' of 'the armed man'—the one which William had remitted to Pope Alexander—had fallen. There are strong grounds for thinking that the reliquary on which Earl Harold had allegedly sworn, and which Duke William had worn around his neck at Hastings, was bequeathed to the church by its founder. With this singular exception, however, English churches had a continuous life over the Conquest. True, their estates might have suffered depredations, often at the hands of other churches: the extant land pleas of the 1070s and 1080s seem to have been concerned with resolving the resulting disputes. But these were losses or gains on the margins. Pre- and post-Conquest prelates held, by and large, the same estates, because they were the estates of the churches over which the prelates presided.

By contrast, as we have seen, the lay estates of Edwardian England did not survive. Indeed, they were dismembered. Domesday Book, regardless of its fiction of continuity, can be made to reveal as much. Post-Conquest lay tenancies-in-chief were not created all at once, and in their final form. They were repeatedly reconfigured, and sometimes suppressed altogether. Some Norman tenants-in-chief, like another son of William fitzOsbern, Roger, earl of Hereford, or the king's uterine brother, Odo, bishop of Bayeux and earl of Kent, had been dispossessed for disloyalty. Forfeiture by those exceptional Englishmen who were initially allowed to survive and to redeem their lands from the king, was a piecemeal process. With each rebellion, more were picked off. Waltheof, a surviving Englishman who was made earl of Northumbria by the Conqueror in 1072, was dispossessed in 1075 for his alleged complicity in the revolt of that year, the last English one of the reign (which was also the occasion for Roger of Hereford's dispossession). Lay tenancies in chief were spatchcocked together in fits and starts. For instance, Henry de Ferrers, later a Domesday commissioner on the West Midlands circuit, received his in at least five successive tranches, one of which, given c. 1071, had previously been held by another Norman. In practical terms, it is impossible to conceive of Henry doing homage to the king on each successive occasion, as the Conqueror augmented his estates. We know that, until roughly 1100, quotas of knight service were revised to take account of such changes on the same arbitrary basis as the original quotas were imposed: the revised quotas continued to be divisible by five. But quotas could be recalibrated centrally, at the stroke of a quill. Such adjustments did not require a personal meeting at which a ceremony would take place.

When, conversely, English laymen submitted to the Conqueror, and redeemed their lands from him, William of Poitiers emphasizes that they 'surrendered themselves and all their possessions' to the king, and that the king accepted their oaths of fidelity and 'restored to them all that they had possessed'. Allegedly Stigand, like that perfidious English archetype Harold before him, had 'given himself with his hands'. Englishmen were used to commending themselves to lords, almost certainly in this way; but commendation in Old England created a bond which was solely personal, not tenurial too. Ironically enough, Domesday Book provides the most extensive evidence for this category of Old English lordship, which it terms 'mere commendation'. William of Poitiers never uses the term *homagium*. It first appears in the 1080s; and even if he had known it, he would have avoided it, because, as we have seen, his classical pretensions made him stick strictly to antique vocabulary. But he seems to have envisaged Englishmen submitting to the Conqueror, and being confirmed by him in their lands, when they placed their hands between his. He saw them as doing homage before there was a substantive term for it.

It appears, then, that surviving Edwardian prelates as well as new appointments did homage to the Conqueror for the lands of their churches. Surviving English laymen perhaps also did homage when they redeemed their lands from the king. But it seems unlikely that the new French tenants, who received estates defined in terms of the rights of *antecessores*, did homage for each grant they received. In this respect, Eadmer's assumption that what had been true of ecclesiastical tenancies-in-chief had also been true of lay tenancies-in-chief oversimplifies, because the latter were not existing Edwardian estates re-granted on different terms. They were entirely new confections, many of which were rejigged, often several times. Of course, many Norman settlers would have placed their hands between those of the duke long ago in Normandy. This was, after all, the traditional way in which succession to the duchy was arranged. In 1067, and on several subsequent occasions, the Conqueror had instructed the Norman magnates to do so to his eldest son and chosen successor as duke, Robert Curthose. But as these prospective succession arrangements reveal, homage in Normandy created no tenurial bond between lord and man. In that respect, there was a partial parallel with Old English 'mere commendation'. Yet as both William of Poitiers and Eadmer recognized, in conquered

England it did, apparently from the start. This meant that those French laymen who had not done homage to the king for the lands which he had given them in England would have been curiously anomalous.

The anomaly was resolved on 1 August 1086 at Salisbury. According to the royal courtier who was by then keeping up the only surviving version of the *Anglo-Saxon Chronicle*, the so-called Peterborough chronicle, 'his counsellors came to [the king] there, and all land-holding men of any account throughout England, whosesoever men they were, and they all bowed to him and became his men and swore oaths of fealty to him, that they would remain faithful to him against all other men.' Like many entries in the *Chronicle*, this is cryptic; but it seems to describe in non-technical vernacular the king receiving homage and fealty not only from tenants-in-chief, but also from at least some subtenants. In the early 12th century, Henry of Huntingdon interpreted it to include not just some particularly important subtenants, but all landholders.

The only precedent for a grand occasion at Salisbury had occurred in early 1070, when, according to Orderic Vitalis drawing on the lost ending of William of Poitiers, the king had 'distributed lavish rewards' there to those who had helped him to suppress recent rebellions. It is unclear whether these 'rewards' for the harriers of the North included land, and whether the recipients made any formal submission to the king in return. But perhaps this event was one reason why the Conqueror selected Salisbury for the ceremony to be held, unprecedentedly, at Lammas—'Loaf-mass'—the feast of the first fruits of the harvest, in 1086. Other considerations may have included the hilltop site, which allowed plenty of space for mustering large numbers; the fact that six Roman roads radiated from the prehistoric fortification in which the king's castle had been constructed; and Salisbury's post-Conquest role, soon second only to Winchester, in royal government.

In keeping with Salisbury's new role as a major administrative centre, it was probably also there that the circuit returns from the Domesday Survey were collated and recast into the final form which they assumed in the Book. The *Liber Exoniensis*, the draft return for the southwestern circuit, was certainly written in the cathedral *scriptorium*. This is no coincidence. The Survey had been conceived at the gathering of the traditional Christmas court at Gloucester in 1085 with, presumably, a very tight timetable, if everything was to be accomplished in seven months. According to the *Chronicle*, the 'writings' produced by this elaborate enterprise 'were brought to [the king] afterwards'. The most convenient location for such a presentation was where they were written, and the date must have been set well in advance, when

10. **Old Sarum Cathedral, which became redundant in the twelfth century, viewed from the ramparts of the king's castle. Some of the manuscripts associated with the Domesday Survey were written in its *scriptorium*; it seems likely that the returns were collated and redrafted here. They were presented to King William, probably on Lammas Day (1 August) 1086, when 'all landholding men of any account' did homage to him 'at Salisbury'**

'all landholding men of any account throughout England' were summoned there. A late addition found in *Liber Exoniensis*, and copied verbatim in Domesday Book itself, records that the king had granted a parcel of land to Walkelin, bishop of Winchester 'as [the king] acknowledged at Salisbury in the hearing of the bishop of Durham, whom he instructed that the grant should be entered in his writings (*breves*).' William of St Calais, bishop of Durham, was the mastermind behind the whole Survey. (That his successor was Ranulf Flambard confirms that Durham had become a see reserved for mandarins.) This entry, made in the king's 'writings' by his command at Salisbury, is best explained as the record of an oral amendment he made when he received those 'writings', which must have included *Liber Exoniensis*. The hand in which the entry is made appears nowhere else in the manuscript. Domesday Book itself had not yet been written up in its final form, but the returns of the circuits were certainly available to the king in Salisbury on 1 August, when homage was done and oaths sworn to him on a scale which appears to have been unprecedented.

The Conqueror seems to have planned from the Survey's inception that its completion would intersect with the ceremony at Salisbury. This decision must have been taken during the 'deep speech' which, according to the probably eye-witness author of the *Chronicle*, the king had held with his counsellors at Christmas 1085. The (English) title Domesday Book—the book of final or last judgement, as it was rendered by Henry II's treasurer in the 1180s—first appears much later; but the Old English word *boc* (diploma or charter) translates what it was known as almost from the beginning, by the king's chancery and others: 'the king's charter' or 'the original (*autentica*) *cartula* of the king'. This is a plausible description of Domesday Book. It recorded, twenty years after the Conquest, the lands—or first fruits—for which many lay French settlers now did homage to the king for the first time. It did so comprehensively, for the whole kingdom (with the exception of certain parts which the Old English governmental system had not yet reached, which were therefore inaccessible to the Survey; and, for different reasons, London and Winchester). It attempted to resolve as many disputed claims as possible, with intractable ones consigned to appendices for later resolution. Or as Henry II's treasurer put it in the anachronistic, self-consciously Romanesque language of the late 12th century: 'A careful survey of the whole country was made in order that every man be content with his own rights and not encroach unpunished on those of others.'

The planned conjunction of the completion of the Survey with the ceremony at Salisbury thus put the lay tenants-in-chief who had come over with the Conqueror, or subsequently, on the same footing as ecclesiastical ones and the few survivors from the time of King Edward. The precariousness of that shared relationship with the king is revealed by the fact that if the king's homagers thought in 1086 that the recording of their lands in Domesday would afford them, and perhaps their heirs, a greater security of tenure in England, they were soon to be disabused of that naïve misapprehension. William Rufus (1087–1100) and Henry I (1100–35) continued to exploit the powers which precarious dependence gave them, despite undertakings they gave at moments of weakness to be better lords to their men. Henry I was particularly disparaging about his brother and predecessor when seeking to succeed him. Estates could be forfeited for disloyalty; vast sums, termed reliefs, could be screwed out of heirs in return for the king condescending to accept their homage, and thereby to re-grant an ancestor's estate. Domesday Book facilitated royal exploitation of precariousness. So far as the tenants-in-chief were concerned, the Book turned out not only not to be worth the parchment it was written on, it exposed them to the untrammeled efficiency of royal exaction by hard-nosed bureaucrats like Ranulf Flambard. For that very reason, of course, it was invaluable to the royal administration. Whichever royal counsellor it was who hit on Lammas Day as the deadline must have taken a rueful satisfaction in its ironic appropriateness.

Where the subtenants were concerned, however, it was a different matter. By specifying that those who did homage and swore fealty to the king at Salisbury included some who were already the men of other men, the author of the *Anglo-Saxon Chronicle* made it quite clear that the king established direct, formal bonds with the tenants of his tenants-in-chief. We know that the king had previously intervened *ad hoc* to protect subtenants: for instance, he had ordered the abbot of Abingdon to provide Hermer, a mercenary knight formerly in the abbot's employ, with a life tenancy as a sort of disability pension, after Hermer's hands were chopped off by pirates in the English Channel. But what happened at Salisbury was not an *ad hoc* royal response to an individual's appeal for help; it appears to have been widespread, perhaps even systematic, and it happened at the king's instigation.

It is impossible to define what the *Anglo-Saxon Chronicle* meant by a subtenant 'of any account'; but the fact that Domesday Book is, to say the least, lackadaisical about recording subtenants suggests that, where they were concerned, the connection between the Book and the ceremony at Salisbury was less intimate. Perhaps they were the exceptional subtenants who are recorded by name in the Book, though there is no way of proving this. Doubtless William of St Calais, as one might expect of an adroit bureaucrat, was trying to kill any number of birds with these two stones. The import of the direct connection established between king and subtenants was, ironically enough, brought home to the bishop himself, early in the next reign. His vassals sided with William Rufus, and against him, when the new king deprived him of his bishopric in 1088. The community of interest created between king and subtenants at Salisbury means that it is quite misleading to describe post-Conquest England as a feudal pyramid, a cliché beloved of textbooks. That community of interest had a very important future. It explains, for instance, the design of the new common law procedures of Henry II's reign (1154–89), in which he sought to circumscribe the freedom of action of tenants-in-chief over their men, whereas he, as king, remained comparatively unrestricted in his exercise of his lordly powers over his tenants-in-chief.

Eadmer may have oversimplified and got some of the details wrong. But as he disarmingly pleaded, he was writing ecclesiastical history. It was not his business to write about commensurate changes in secular affairs. He could only drop hints. As with any of the great Roman historians, it is as important to read between his lines as the lines themselves. Domesday Book and what modern historians have misleadingly termed the 'oath of Salisbury' can be used to supply the deficit. They reveal that he had identified the most important novelty of the Conquest with the perspicacity praised by William of Malmesbury. It was homage which came to constitute that relationship between royal lord and vassal on which everything else depended, and in imitation of that defining archetype, the relationship between every other lord and his men. In the case of laymen, homage elided the distinction between personal lordship and land tenure which Domesday Book itself reveals was common in Old England; in the case of prelates, it elided the distinction between the tenure of ecclesiastical office and the tenure of ecclesiastical land. In both cases, it did so for the same reason: the post-Conquest king's position as the fount of all tenure; or in Eadmer's succinct, Roman phrase, the ruler's 'nod'.

Chapter 4
The Romanesque rebuilding of England

There was one exception to the rule that all major Old English churches were razed to the ground in the first fifty years after the Conquest: Westminster Abbey, where the Conqueror had been made king on Christmas Day 1066. The *Life* of Edward the Confessor, commissioned by his queen, gives an exultant description of the new church which Edward built there to

11. Bayeux Tapestry: the consecration of Edward the Confessor's still incomplete Romanesque abbey church at Westminster at Christmas 1065. Excavations have established that the architectural detail is probably accurate

replace the existing one. This description justifies William of Malmesbury's later statements that the church was constructed in 'a new manner of building'; a 'manner of design that he was the first to have used in England, and that nowadays almost everyone tries to imitate at great expense'. The description of the church in the *Life*, written not long after its consecration at Christmas 1065 while still incomplete, its depiction in that incomplete state in the Bayeux Tapestry, and archaeological excavations all confirm that it was built in the Romanesque style then in vogue on the continent.

There are very close similarities between Edward's Westminster and the new abbey church at Jumièges, which was consecrated during King William's triumphal return to Normandy in the spring of 1067. Most tellingly, the alternating pattern of piers in the nave is found in these two buildings and nowhere else. These similarities have been attributed to the influence of Robert, sometime abbot of Jumièges. Shortly after Edward's accession as king, and not long before the rebuilding of Westminster Abbey began, he had made Robert bishop of London. The crisis triggered by Robert's translation to Canterbury in 1051 was resolved when he fled back to Jumièges for good in September 1052. In the meantime, according to the *Life*, he had been the king's chief counsellor 'for good or ill'; the author's enthusiastic description of the new abbey church would suggest that it would fall into the former category.

It is not clear whether the architect of Jumièges was commissioned, at Bishop Robert's instigation, to design the much grander building just outside London, or whether Robert took with him drawings of Westminster as well as liturgical books—the so-called *Missal of Robert of Jumieges*—when he fled back to his abbey in 1052. (An inscription at the end of the book, probably in Robert's hand, records the donation.) On balance, the former seems more likely, partly because the new church at Jumièges was started c. 1040, before Westminster. Whichever

12. Rouen, Bibliothèque municipale MS. Y, fo. 36. This richly illustrated English sacramentary was given to Jumieges Abbey by Robert, abbot of Jumièges (1037–44), bishop of London (1044–51), and briefly archbishop of Canterbury (1051–2). This illumination depicts the journey of the *magi*. An inscription, probably in Robert's hand, records that he gave the book while he was bishop of London, and invoked divine retribution on anyone who might steal it. At a later date, perhaps after he had sought refuge at Jumièges in 1052, he added similar imprecations against those who took any of his other gifts

was the case, the names of some of the masons employed at Westminster are recorded in Edward the Confessor's writs: Leofsi Duddesunu, Godwin Gretsyd, and Teinfrith, the king's 'church wright', or master mason. These names are not Norman, but apparently English and, in Teinfrith's case, German. The employment of a German as master mason would make sense. The scale of Westminster Abbey was so much grander than anything in Normandy that it bears comparison only with the huge Romanesque cathedrals of contemporary Germany, such as Speyer (1030–61).

According to the *Life*, King Edward had planned from the start that he would be buried in this new church. If so, he envisaged it as replacing the 10th-century Old Minster at Winchester, where he had been anointed as king, and where many of his predecessors had been interred. Such grandiose aspirations would have made the huge churches of imperial Germany a suitable model, at least with respect to size. They were fitting venues for royal ceremonial. We know from the appointments Edward made to his writing office and to English churches that he was by no means averse to importing foreign know how, rather than relying on native talent. In that respect, his many years of exile in Normandy had had a profound influence on him. Many of those he appointed, like Regenbald and Giso, were, however, not Normans, but Germans from Lotharingia.

Edward the Confessor's Westminster Abbey is, therefore, a text-book example of an exception proving the rule. It was the outstanding manifestation of that Edwardian aping of continental building which, on a more mundane level, produced a small number of foreign-style castles in the Welsh bad lands, built by a few Norman lords whom the king had invited to England as lay counterparts to the likes of Robert of Jumièges. As the *Life* makes clear, at Westminster no expense had been spared. But a huge, recent outlay was not in itself enough to save a church from rebuilding after 1066. The abbey of Gloucester, for instance, was extensively remodeled in the late 1050s in order to provide a fitting venue for Christmas crown-wearings, at which the king would have liturgical acclamations—*laudes*—sung to him. The round of triannual crown-wearing which, according to the *Anglo-Saxon Chronicle*, the Conqueror maintained so sedulously seems to have started, or at least to have been regularized, under Edward the Confessor. It was masterminded by Ealdred, then bishop of Worcester (and later, of course, archbishop of York), who had witnessed such regal ceremonies in Germany in the 1050s, imported liturgical books from Germany into England, and in whose diocese Gloucester Abbey was located. Ealdred was the closest thing Edwardian England had to a consultant on royal ceremonial. His putative role would explain why Gloucester should become the third location for annual crown-wearings, along with the more obviously predictable Winchester and Westminster, where the grand, new abbey church was already under construction.

But Gloucester's recent, and presumably splendid, refurbishment did not save it after the Conquest. Redevelopment began four years after the celebrated 'deep speech' of Christmas 1085 (which may have taken place in the existing chapter house, some of which is thought to predate the rebuilding). The reason often given for rebuilding here, as in many other locations, was fire. We can still see its effects on the lower parts of the walls of the chapter house, which nevertheless survive. The fire of 1122 calcinated the massive columns in the new nave, but did not destroy them. Other than roofs, most elements of most large Old English churches were built of stone, and it requires extraordinarily intense heat to make stone fragment and crumble. Fires could be exploited as an excuse for rebuilding; but as at already rebuilt Romanesque Gloucester after 1122, they did not have to be exploited in that way. In 1113, the roof of the new Romanesque cathedral at Worcester was gutted by fire. According to William of Malmesbury, 'Rafters as big as whole trees fell charred to the floor.' But Bishop Wulfstan's tomb escaped even smuts and ash; the rush matting on which pilgrims knelt in front of it was unharmed. Whatever the extent of the damage elsewhere in the building, no-one contemplated demolishing Wulfstan's new cathedral and starting again.

What saved Westminster Abbey was not that it was new, or opulent, or massive by any standards, or that it escaped a serious fire, but that Edward the Confessor was buried there, and William the Conqueror was anointed there. The *laudes* which Ealdred had specially composed for the coronation of Queen Matilda at Whitsun 1068 had been sung there (when the king had issued his charter in favour of Giso of Wells); they survive in a liturgical handbook of Ealdred's which also includes material he imported from Germany. According to William of Malmesbury, 'the custom grew up…that in memory of Edward's burial place, those who were about to rule should receive the royal crown there'. King William must have completed it with this purpose in mind. It was

13. Gloucester Cathedral (then Abbey), Chapter House: although this was later substantially rebuilt, the lower parts of the walls remain from the building in which the Conqueror had 'deep speech' with his *witan* at Christmas 1085, and took the decision to carry out the Domesday Survey

a unique architectural manifestation of the façade of continuity, and it established, as William of Malmesbury said, a model for the rebuilding of all other major English churches.

Whereas Westminster Abbey was cherished, no other major English church seems to have survived the first fifty years. It used to be claimed that Harold's foundation of Holy Cross, Waltham—his alleged place of burial—was also spared, as if this betrayed on the part of the victors a twinge of conscience akin to that expressed in the careful location of the high altar of the penitential foundation at Battle on the very spot where King Harold had fallen. But recent archaeological evidence has demonstrated beyond doubt that this church was no exception to the programme of blanket rebuilding. The church which Earl Harold had known, like everywhere else except Westminster, was not allowed to survive.

According to William of Malmesbury, who claimed to have had the story from his friend Prior Nicholas of Worcester, an eye-witness, Bishop Wulfstan had wept over the demolition of the old cathedral at Worcester. Some also said that the bishop had prophesied the fire of 1113, though William regarded the evidence as less conclusive. But we have already seen that these were sanctimonious, crocodile tears. Wulfstan, a wily clerical operator, had increased the number of monks at Worcester from 12 to 50, and wanted spanking-new buildings commensurate with this renewal of ecclesiastical life in his diocese. A contemporary charter suggests that he was, as we might expect if it were not for Prior Nicholas's improving anecdote, the prime mover in the building project. Æthelwig, abbot of Evesham, that other great survivor from the hierarchy of Edward the Confessor's reign, did not initiate the rebuilding of his church. But this was not because he was sentimentally reluctant to do so. Rather, it was because he died too soon, in 1078. By then, he had expanded the number of brethren from 12 to 36, and, according to the *Evesham History*, 'left five caskets full of silver for the erection of the new church which he had planned to build'. It was his successor Walter, a former monk of Cerisy, a pupil and latterly chaplain of Lanfranc, who implemented Æthelwig's plan. 'Delighted by recent architecture, he began the church, and gradually destroyed the ancient building, which at that time stood out amongst the most beautiful in England. The remains, it is a marvel to relate, of this great work of antiquity were heaped up together in the one crypt.' A shortage of building materials soon required the recovery of some of this discarded stone for re-use in the new church. Eventually, lack of resources impelled Abbot Walter to send two monks out on a fund raising expedition, using the relics of St Ecgwine to arouse enthusiasm. It would seem, then, that Ecgwine's relics had not, like assorted saints at Malmesbury under Abbot Warin, been thrown into the skip along with the shattered debris from this outstandingly beautiful Old English church. Walter did, on Lanfranc's advice, subject the bones of several Evesham saints to an ordeal by fire; but they passed, and were then restored. Yet if Walter was treating Ecgwine's relics with reverence, it was an entrepreneurial reverence. They were pressed into service of the new building project. All available resources were, it seems: Domesday Book records, in the words of long-suffering hundredal jurors, that the abbot's manor of Offenham had enough oxen for one plough, 'but they haul stone for the church'.

The *Evesham History*'s account of Abbot Walter's activities verges on sarcasm; the author of a 12th-century work now known as *De abbatibus Abendonie* was more straightforward about Abbot Adelelm, a monk from Jumièges who was substituted in 1071 for Abbot Ealdred (who was locked up for the rest of his life, in the custody of Walkelin of Winchester). Adelelm treated the revered Abingdon saints, Abbot Æthelwold (954–63) and Edward, king and martyr (d. 978), with contempt: 'One day when he sat at table with his relatives and cronies, he ridiculed St Æthelwold and his works, saying that the church of English peasants ought not to stand, but be destroyed. After dinner, he rose from table and went out to attend an urgent need; there he cried out wretchedly. When his attendants ran up they found him dead'. Undignified death in a privy had been a fitting end for a tyrant since antiquity; here it was Adelelm's comeuppance for sacrilegious disrespect shown to English saints and their church. This is not, however, the story told in the major history of the house, *The History of the Church of Abingdon*, although that story is not incompatible with it. The *History* simply recorded that Abbot Adelelm had amassed sufficient resources to fund the rebuilding, but had died suddenly in 1083 when it was still in train. What is clear is that any resentment felt by the English at the wholesale destruction of their architectural relics did nothing to slow the process of rebuilding at Abingdon, as elsewhere. William of Malmesbury felt obliged to report 'the grumbles of those who said it would be better to preserve the old foundations in their former state than to rob them to build new ones while they fell into ruins'. But grumbles were no more than an ineffectual lament for a world which was being systematically obliterated. They might afford a quiet, bitter solace to the disaffected, but they achieved nothing.

The process of rebuilding was prosecuted with a zeal which sometimes verged on profligate recklessness. Thus Abbot Thurstan of Glastonbury, the perpetrator of the atrocity of 1083 in which monks were cut down on the high altar for resisting his imposition of foreign liturgy, also undertook the rebuilding of the abbey. Glastonbury was the richest abbey in Old England, and the burial place of King Edgar, whose reign was viewed by Eadmer and others as the apogee of English history. The subsequent, sharp decline, manifest in Cnut's takeover, had reached its nadir in the Norman Conquest. It had been a just punishment for English complicity in the assassination of Edward the Martyr (whose relics Abbot Adelelm of Abingdon treated as so much detritus). Dunstan, archbishop of Canterbury under Edgar, had previously been abbot of Glastonbury. As was often the case with major Old English foundations, there were several churches at

Glastonbury, built in a line on an east-west axis. The oldest, called 'Ealdchirche' by the English, had allegedly been built of wattle by twelve disciples of the apostles Philip and James, and was later extended in wood; the newest, built on to the 'Ealdchirche' by King Ine of Wessex in the 8th century, had been greatly extended by Dunstan in the tenth. William of Malmesbury's description of the four churches evokes the English sense that the very buildings were to be cherished as relics. Whenever possible, old churches were extended or adapted. When this was impossible, they were not demolished, but reverently preserved. In William of Malmesbury's view, Glastonbury Abbey, embodied in its four churches, had been 'redolent with divine sanctity'. Thurstan planned to sweep all these sacred buildings away. He treated them with an irreverent insensitivity akin to that which left the wooden cross above the high altar in Ine's church bristling with arrows, and which grievously wounded a silver crucifix used as a shield by one of the monks. The miraculous effusion of blood from the silver figure of Christ had mingled with that of the slain monks on the altar steps.

The new church was so ambitious in scale that it was still 'unfinished'—which must mean that even its east end was incomplete—when Herluin, another monk of St-Étienne, Caen, succeeded Thurstan as abbot in 1101. Rather than complete the project, however, Herluin decided that that it was not grand enough, given the resources of the abbey. He had the new church, too, razed to the ground, and started again from scratch, on an even more opulent scale. The archaeological record confirms William of Malmesbury's account. He specifies the expenditure on Abbot Herluin's rebuilding of the rebuilding, perhaps because his *De antiquitate Glastonie ecclesie* had been commissioned by the current abbot, who required such details to be recorded, or perhaps to imply vulgarity, or perhaps both: Herluin had spent £480 on the church and 70 marks on 'an image and a cross'. In view of William's accounts of the atrocity in 1083, the latter detail must be pointed. Could the expenditure of such a colossal sum compensate for the injuries inflicted on the rood and crucifix by the arrows of Abbot Thurstan's men-at-arms?

Glastonbury's experience of Norman imposition of liturgical conformity was exceptionally violent. The notoriety of the incident obliged the Conqueror himself to intervene. Abbot Thurstan was sent back to Caen for a time; and the recalcitrant monks were dispersed like troublemakers around other monasteries. The last thing the king would have wanted was for Glastonbury Abbey to become a centre of English resentment, and potentially of resistance. Other houses also had foreign liturgy forced down their throats, if not under a hail of arrows. Walcher, a monk of Liège, was made bishop of Durham in 1072, his English predecessor having been deposed and imprisoned (and dying not long afterwards, allegedly on hunger strike). One aspect of Bishop Walcher's attempt to import Norman civilization to the North was the imposition of foreign liturgical practice on the Durham clerks. His assassination in 1080 was provoked not by the enforcement of new liturgical practices, but by the behaviour of his knights. It demonstrated that there were still limits to the effectiveness of Norman power in the North, even after the harrying.

The gross inefficiency, or incompetence, or profligacy on the part of Abbots Thurstan and Herluin with respect to the planning of new buildings at Glastonbury is likewise not unparalleled. At Old Sarum, celebrated by English historians for reasons other than its ruins, the king built a castle within the prehistoric earthworks; construction had probably begun by the time he distributed 'lavish rewards' to his followers there in 1070, as reported by Orderic Vitalis. In 1075, Bishop Heremann of Sherborne, like Giso and Regenbald a Lotharingian and a former chaplain of Edward the Confessor, moved his see to Old Sarum, 'a castle in place of a city, on a hill top and mightily walled'.

This was the second post-Conquest instance of that policy, implemented so enthusiastically under William the Conqueror, of moving sees away from the rural locations which had been a distinctively English legacy of the conversion, into cities, in accordance with practice elsewhere in western Europe. But in the case of Old Sarum, of course, there was at this stage no city, only a new centre of royal government. As the writing of the *Liber Exoniensis* demonstrates, the administration of the conquered kingdom could be greatly facilitated by the proximity of a cathedral *scriptorium*—and this one was soon acknowledged as the most intellectually distinguished in the kingdom. Tax surveys carried out in 1084–5 and appended to the *Liber Exoniensis* were also copied there. It was no accident that Heremann, after successfully evading Lanfranc's attempt to force him into early retirement in 1072, was succeeded as bishop by Osmund, the king's chancellor, in 1079. The cathedral was built within the bailey of the king's castle, which meant that there were severe limitations on size. It is probably for this reason, rather than initial modesty on Bishop Hermann's part, that the new church was as unpretentious in style as it was in scale.

Remigius, a former monk of Fécamp who had disregarded his priestly obligations in order to fight at Hastings, was made bishop of Dorchester in 1067. In 1072, he had moved his see to Lincoln, at the opposite, insecure, northern end of his large diocese. There he had begun the construction of a massive new cathedral, the west work of which had many of the characteristics of a fortification, as befitted a major building project in the newly harried, but still insecure, North. Henry of Huntingdon, who knew it well, described it as 'a strong church in a strong place, and a beautiful church in a beautiful place: invincible to enemies as suited the times'. At Old Sarum, by contrast, the site of the relocated see left little scope for innovation or grandeur.

In the 12th century, Peter of Blois described Old Sarum Cathedral as 'an ark of God shut up in a temple of Baal'. Salisbury, like Durham after the assassination of Bishop Walcher, became a see reserved for senior officiants in the (post-Conquest) cult of Baal.

Henry I's chancellor, Roger, was made bishop in 1102. Evidently he decided that the meanest of the new English cathedrals was no longer suitable for someone of his august station. He therefore set about enlarging it. William of Malmesbury commented, with some exaggeration: 'He made a new church of Salisbury and furnished it with ornaments, so that it yields to none in England, and exceeds many...'. Bishop Roger's model was Bishop Walkelin's Winchester; but however imposing the model, the location at Old Sarum made it impossible to build something commensurate with Roger's pretensions. In the early 13th century, his remodelled cathedral was made redundant, and a third cathedral was built on the river floodplain below Old Sarum, at the centre of what became the new, planned city of Salisbury. It is a testimony to the scale and permanence of the Norman rebuilding of English churches that this was the first new cathedral to be built subsequently, and the last one prior to Sir Christopher Wren's St Paul's (which replaced the Romanesque cathedral destroyed in the Great Fire of London of 1666). The history of Old Sarum Cathedral, like that of Glastonbury Abbey, is, however, a testimony to the fact that many of the rebuilding projects initiated so comprehensively and with such intemperate urgency were ill thought-out, and could therefore prove to be ephemeral.

Often, they were also shoddily executed. At Old Sarum, the bell tower blew down just five days after Bishop Osmund had consecrated the new cathedral in 1092. Indeed, new towers fell like ninepins all across England. Most famously, Winchester Cathedral's collapsed in 1107—because, it was believed, King William Rufus, that infamous plunderer of vacant churches and wearer of fancy boots, was buried beneath it. Towers also fell at Abingdon (1091), Gloucester (end of the 11th century), Ely (1111), Worcester (1175), Evesham (1210), and Lincoln (1240), to name only churches already discussed. Either England was then afflicted by hurricanes of a severity and frequency which we, in an era of supposedly extreme weather conditions, can scarcely imagine, or these buildings were poorly constructed. The number of collapses attributed to earthquakes also strains credibility: the *Annales Monastici* alone record fifteen in the period 1076–1201. Any tremors felt are more likely to have been the consequence than the cause of collapse.

It may be that the 11th- and 12th-century architects were simply incapable of the mathematical calculations needed to design arches, vaulting, and buttresses which would work. But those in charge of the building operations must have planned in great detail to ensure that the vast numbers of precision-cut pieces of stone were delivered on time to be assembled on site. This would suggest that they were capable of making the requisite structural calculations too. So would the fact that the ratio between the length of a side of the cloister and the length of the nave is demonstrably one to the square root of two in churches where both the length of original nave and the dimensions of the original cloister (where the foundation was not a secular one) can still be established. This was the case at Westminster Abbey (though interestingly not at Jumièges), confirming William of Malmesbury's claim that it was a model for subsequent Romanesque churches in England. At St Albans and Norwich this is also the ratio between the height of the lantern and the top of the tower. The same proportion governs the relation between the interior and exterior width of the nave, thus determining the thickness of the walls; and so on. This architectonic proportion, according to which all parts of the building are related to each other, was not simply plucked out of the air. It is the proportion between the side of a square and its diagonal; but this does not mean that it was determined by some universal practical imperative, which governed all church building. It was perhaps derived ultimately, or even directly, from the ancient Roman architect Vitruvius. Vitruvius's influence was profound. His stipulation that Ionic columns must have 24 flutes also explains why the westernmost columns in Durham Cathedral have 24 flutes. Although the square root of two ratio is found in some pre-Conquest English and some contemporary German churches, it is rare in Normandy. It is virtually universal in conquered England.

Those who designed these churches were not, therefore, innumerate. The more prudent might have erred on the side of caution in calculating loads, stresses, and strains. Well they might, given that they were building on a scale for which their Norman experience—if they had any—would not have equipped them. They were pushing forward into unexplored space, architecturally speaking. But most seem to have been capable of making such calculations, otherwise the buildings could not have been put up at all. Where they ran into trouble was with foundations, which frequently turned out to be catastrophically inadequate (and on which Vitruvius offered no guidance). Some of the less catastrophic consequences, for instance in Abbot Serlo's rebuilding of Ealdred's recently remodeled Gloucester Abbey, are still with us: the massive, circular columns in the south aisle of the nave lean away from their northern pairs. Remedial work had to be undertaken in the early 14th century to deal with the subsidence. The more catastrophic ones are self-evidently no longer with us, such as the original tower at the crossing of Winchester Cathedral. William of Malmesbury took the rational view that its collapse had been caused by poor foundations, rather than the proximity of William Rufus's sacrilegious remains. It is no wonder that Bishop William of St Calais began the digging of the foundations for Durham Cathedral on 29 July 1093 with special prayers and a blessing, or that a fortnight later he and the prior, together with Malcolm, king of the Scots, laid the first stones. Even for the empirical man behind the Domesday Survey, divine underpinning was too obvious a precaution to be missed.

Another factor is that perennial English problem, shoddy workmanship. Much of the stonework, particularly in the first churches to be rebuilt, is of poor quality. Later, from the 1090s, there was some improvement. There is, for instance, a very noticeable difference between the standard of the masonry at

Winchester, begun in 1079, and that at Durham, begun in 1093. The stonework at Jumièges and St-Étienne, Caen, both earlier than Winchester, is more akin to the latter than the former, so shoddy workmanship was not a Norman import. Churches begun in England in the first twenty-five years after the Conquest have no mouldings, although these were prominent in Norman buildings. Durham, started in 1093, is the first to have them. Those parts of Ely Abbey built before 1093, when work was stopped at the beginning of an abbatial vacancy, have none, those parts built after 1100, when work recommenced, do. The surviving bits of the original Winchester Cathedral have none, but they feature in the reconstruction which followed the collapse of the tower in 1107. It may therefore be the case that many Romanesque buildings in conquered England were so shoddily constructed and, in the early stages, so unadorned because there were simply not enough skilled masons to mount a building campaign on the scale required by the kingdom's new rulers and the prelates they imported. It was another early manifestation of that other familiar English problem: the skill shortage. Eventually, the supply of masons increased. Alternatively, it has been suggested that mouldings were avoided immediately after the Conquest because they were considered an indigenous feature, and the Normans were very concerned to differentiate the new architecture from English traditions. But this interpretation is undermined by the sloppiness of craftsmanship evident in the initial building boom. William of Malmesbury's eulogy on the masonry in Roger of Salisbury's buildings at Malmesbury (which probably refers to the castle, with which William must have been very familiar) and Old Sarum in the 1120s suggests that work of this quality was still quite exceptional: 'the courses of stone are laid so exactly that the joints defy inspection and give the whole wall the appearance of a single rock face'.

In terms of appearance, as opposed to structural soundness, the quality of masonry did not matter as much as William of Malmesbury's admiring description implies. For not only were the interiors of these churches painted, so were the exteriors. A few surviving fragments indicate that a typical interior featured a profusion of figurative cycles, mainly depicting scenes from scripture (and matched in the stained-glass windows). Some idea of the impressiveness of these paintings is given by the much smaller scale ones in out-of-the-way parish churches which escaped the attentions of religious fanatics in the 16th and 17th centuries. Of those at Canterbury Cathedral, William of Malmesbury wrote: 'In the multi-coloured paintings remarkable artistic skill, enhancing the splendour of the pigments, quite carried the heart away; and the charm of beauty aroused the eyes towards the panelled ceiling.' An impression of the effect is given by the 19th-century painted wooden ceiling at Ely (parts of a 13th-century example survive at Peterborough). But it was of course not possible to cover every square inch of interior surfaces in this way. Where there were carved features, they were simply highlighted with paint; but where the masonry was plain, it was whitewashed, with the lines of mortar picked out in red.

This was the case not only inside the churches, but outside. Exterior paintwork was not confined to the portals. For obvious reasons, even less evidence of this sort of exterior paintwork survives; but there is some on the exterior of the south transept at York Minster, which had been started by Archbishop Thomas in 1080. That the painted red mortar lines are only very roughly related to the real mortar might on occasion have been contrived to conceal botched jobs by incompetent masons, but in most cases the paintwork is less regular than the stonework which lies beneath. This suggests that the paintwork was not for the most part a disguise, but rather that paintwork of one sort or another must cover all the masonry for a church to be considered complete. When, in the first few years after the Conquest, castles were thrown up at great speed using earth, stone, and timber (as depicted in the Bayeux Tapestry), the exteriors may have been painted to look like stone. For obvious reasons, little evidence of this practice survives; but there are some traces of exterior painted stucco at Geoffrey de Mandeville's wooden castle of the 1140s at South Mimms, Hertfordshire. If this practice was widespread earlier on, it is a telling example of Norman faith in gimcrackery. The Normans did not share the modern obsession with being true to their materials, or even, it seems, our more long-standing appreciation of the colour and texture of stone. On the contrary, the important thing was the impression given by the veneer of paint, not the underlying substance. The Normans were great believers in veneers of one sort or another.

It is very difficult for us to clear our minds of Wordsworth's re-echoing of Shakespeare's 'bare, ruin'd choirs', and to substitute this brash profusion of colour. William of Malmesbury's account of the effect on observers corroborates that given earlier by Goscelin of St Bertin, a Fleming in the household of Bishop Heremann of Sherborne from 1058. He was commissioned to write many hagiographies in late 11th-century England, including (probably) the *Life of Edward the Confessor*. His work elicited another of William's very rare compliments: in William's view, Goscelin was second only to Bede in the ranks of English hagiographers. Goscelin complained about the mean and dingy lodgings in which he had been quartered on his arrival in England. Elsewhere he wrote:

> He destroys well who builds something better. A useless little
> man, who takes up little ground, I greatly dislike little buildings
> and, though devoid of resources, propose splendid things. And so,
> if given the means, I would not allow buildings, although much
> esteemed, to stand, unless they were, according to my idea, glorious,
> magnificent, most lofty, most spacious, filled with light and most
> beautiful.

Ostensibly he was discussing the 'most elegant architect' of the heavenly Jerusalem, but his imagination had clearly been fired by what he had seen in England—even, perhaps, by the original Old Sarum, the least splendid of all the new cathedrals. It gave a foretaste of heaven. He had been brought to England to remedy the deficiency in English written records of saints. He was much in demand after the Conquest, as Norman prelates undertook their inquiries into the *bona fides* of supposed English saints. But his concern to preserve this important aspect of English history from oblivion obviously did not extend to the buildings sanctified by the presence of those saints. According to him, there was no question that Romanesque churches were infinitely preferable to what had been obliterated to make way for them. For him, the new style was preferable because of its aesthetic.

We tend to read his description, like William of Malmesbury's, with our own reactions in mind. But what the English would have seen from the outside were massive, stark, bright, uncompromising, foreign structures, which transformed the English landscape out of all recognition. Even inside, the eye would not be allowed to rest on mellow stone if it drifted away from iconographic scenes which sought to focus the mind on the fundamental question of salvation. Instead the worshipper would be confronted by a crude painted counterfeit of the real stonework beneath. We would agree with William and Goscelin about the lofty spaciousness of these buildings, but the beauty which for us inheres in their subtlety and delicacy is to a considerable extent a function of the disappearance over the centuries of that brash make-up which was slapped on to impress contemporaries. For us, the beauty is better revealed as the non-figurative paint is peeled away by time; for them, the paint job was essential to the desired impact of the buildings.

Rebuilding and the relocation of sees

In architecture, as in so much else, subtlety was not the Normans' strong suit. They implemented the Conquest with overwhelming determination and meticulous precision, and therefore with little sensitivity or nuance. I have already mentioned that no English cathedral contains any masonry above ground which dates from before 1066. But of course one of the forces driving the programme of rebuilding was the relocation of sees, and with a relocated see there was no possibility of adapting or integrating elements from the old cathedral—other than relics—into the new. In the case of Dorchester/Lincoln, there was over a hundred miles between the two. It is therefore all the more striking that new cathedrals of relocated sees appear to have made no use of existing churches, in the locations where such buildings must have existed. Furthermore, the old cathedrals were perforce decommissioned when a see was relocated. Bits of Sherborne Cathedral, the predecessor of Old Sarum, were salvaged when a church was refounded there in 1122, after being abandoned for fifty years; but otherwise, at Dorchester, Elmham, Selsey, and Wells, the Old English cathedrals seem simply to have become redundant. No laments have survived for these Old English bare ruined choirs. Elmham's was said to have been still built solely of wood in 1066: it was soon replaced by a Romanesque bishop's chapel, built on the site, probably by Bishop Herbert Losinga, who ended the peripatetic career of the see of Elmham/Thetford by transferring it conclusively to Norwich. The new cathedral buildings were deemed henceforth to be the originals, because they were the locations of the sees, where the translated bones of saints who passed muster were venerated.

This point is made forcefully by the attestations of bishops to an original royal document, the seal of which has probably been lost, issued at Windsor at Whitsun 1072. This ratified an agreement already 'ventilated' at a council held at Easter 'in the royal chapel which is located in the castle', in the presence of the Conqueror and his queen, at Winchester. Doubtless the chapel paintwork was very fresh, for the castle which William fitzOsbern had hurriedly constructed in the spring of 1067 by now included an apsidal stone chapel, with wall paintings and stained glass. The agreement settled the dispute between the archbishops of Canterbury and York concerning Canterbury's claim to 'primacy' over all the churches of Britain—another claim which was in truth a post-Conquest fabrication, but for which pre-Conquest precedents were fabricated with energetic ingenuity. At the opening of the document, the old locations of the sees are given; at the end, where the bishops attest as witnesses, the new locations (though of course several of these proposed relocations were as yet no more than glints in Lanfranc's eye). Thereby continuity was established between the old and the new, and the order of precedence of English sees was maintained, regardless of the relocations.

The only exception was Walkelin of Winchester, who, puzzlingly, attested in order of consecration. This error, if error it was, was corrected in the witness list to the *acta* of the council of London, held in the as yet un-rebuilt St Paul's Cathedral in 1075. The first canon dealt with the seating arrangements. These are always a contentious issue at clerical gatherings, and were fundamental to the purpose of this council, because they were determined by formal precedence. The third canon authorized the relocation of sees from 'villages to cities' (including Sherborne's move to Salisbury). But in these respects, and others, the council was not innovatory: it was simply tidying up decisions made at earlier councils, including those of 1072, for the reform of the English church.

Where the *acta* of 1075 were innovatory was in their careful citation of the canon law authorities on which each canon was based. Most of the authorities cited are derived from Lanfranc's canon law collection, a copy of which he brought to England on his elevation to the see of Canterbury. This copy survives, marked up for ready reference to the authorities cited in Lanfranc's letter collection. So does William of St Calais' personal copy, which he consulted on his knee when on trial for treason in November 1088 at Old Sarum. Perhaps he reflected ruefully on the fickleness of his fortunes since 1 August 1086, when the Survey which he had masterminded had reached its planned consummation on the very same spot. That copies which demonstrably belonged to

14. Canterbury, Dean and Chapter Library, Ch. Ant. A. 2: an original document recording the agreement on the primacy of the see of Canterbury, drawn up at Winchester at Easter 1072. The *signa*, including those of the king, queen, papal legate, Lanfranc, and Wulfstan, bishop of Worcester, all appear to be autograph

15. Cambridge, Peterhouse MS. 74, the copy of Lanfranc's canon law collection which belonged to William of St Calais, bishop of Durham, and the mind behind the Domesday Survey. He referred to it frequently during his trial for treason against William Rufus in 1088

two of the major figures in post-Conquest ecclesiastical history happen to survive is not a miracle. There are eleven extant copies of this collection—an extraordinary survival rate for contemporary manuscripts of a single work from this period—because every cathedral, and most major abbeys, seems to have equipped itself with a copy. It was the indispensable handbook for the reform of English churches, and, indeed, for much else: it establishes, for instance, that an illegitimate successor was in law no successor, and could not therefore be the *antecessor* of any subsequent office holder. In other words, between its covers were to be found many of the canonical authorities which justified and therefore shaped the implementation of the Conquest. Its dissemination throughout all major English churches was less visible than their rebuilding in Romanesque style, but it was just as important a manifestation of their Normanization.

Castles and halls

I have concentrated thus far on ecclesiastical architecture, both because the evidence is much more plentiful than for secular architecture, and because it raises in a far more pointed fashion the questions of continuity which have from 1066 been intrinsic to any assessment of the Conquest. But much of what I have suggested about Romanesque churches is also true of secular buildings. Archaeologists have established that at least some of the smaller early castles, built in haste from earth (for the motte) and timber (for the bailey palisades and any tower), were prefabricated. Hence, probably, the carpenters categorized amongst 'the king's servants' (and tenants) in Domesday Book. This confirms the impression of meticulous preparation for the Conquest given by other sources. As rebellions in the West in 1068, and the North in 1069, were suppressed, so castles were swiftly constructed to pin down these problematic areas. According to Orderic Vitalis, the king's second castle at York was built in 1069 within the space of eight days. These early castles were the pre-eminent instrument of military occupation. They

16. Castle Acre Castle, Norfolk, which belonged to the Warenne family. The original building of the 1070s was the stone house visible in the photograph, around which a much more substantial castle was constructed during Stephen's reign

dominated important urban centres and routes of communication throughout the kingdom. They were modeled on French, not English, buildings. According to the *Anglo-Saxon Chronicle*, when King William returned in triumph to Normandy in March 1067, taking in his train most of the most distinguished English survivors, 'Bishop Odo [his half-brother] and Earl William [fitzOsbern] stayed behind and built castles far and wide

115

throughout this country, and distressed the wretched folk, and always after that it grew much worse.' In addition to Winchester, Domesday Book attributes Berkley, Chepstow, Monmouth, Clifford, Wigmore, and the rebuilding of Ewyas Harold to Earl William (and fails to attribute any castles to Bishop Odo, perhaps because he was in disgrace in 1086). The (English) folk were made wretched not only by the preparatory demolition of urban dwellings repeatedly recorded in Domesday, but also by the forced labour depicted in the Bayeux Tapestry, which was exacted for other construction projects too.

Royal castles were in the custody of royal castellans, but those co-conquerors who received estates from the king also constructed their own castles, mainly in the countryside rather than towns. Initially, they were primarily functional, like William de Warenne's two-storey fortified stone house at Castle Acre, Norfolk, which was probably built in the 1070s. Later they became status symbols too, like the stone keep built on top of the original house at Castle Acre c. 1140, or William d'Albini's magnificent Castle Rising, Norfolk, of the same period, which was militarily of little use, but made an emphatic statement about his wealth and standing. Castle Acre was only of secondary importance to the Warennes—their main seat was at Lewes in Sussex, where they constructed a more conventional castle—but they nevertheless built on a grand scale, and founded a daughter house at Acre to the priory they had already established at Lewes (the first Cluniac house in England). William d'Albini established no monastic house at Castle Rising— his father had founded Wymondham Priory—but construction of the castle did entail the moving of the whole existing village, including the parish church. Both residences were exercises in conspicuous consumption.

When the initial post-Conquest military imperatives slacked off, there was time for some of the impromptu, original royal castles to be rebuilt in stone. Grander ones, such as those initially constructed in Rochester, Winchester, and Colchester, and the southeast corner of the city of London, incorporated surviving Roman masonry from the start. They did so partly because Roman ruins provided ready-made foundations and defences, and perhaps partly because they lent physical substance to the point on which William of Poitiers insists: that William the Conqueror had trumped the Roman conquerors of Britain. In the case of Colchester, for instance, the ruins were of the Temple of Claudius, not of a Roman fort. In practical terms, whoever designed Colchester was greatly constrained by his determination to use of the temple's podium and walls. He was not thinking in terms of practicalities. Roman ruins, made serviceable in the short term, could be integrated with new building in stone later on, as happened in London, where the White Tower—the name is late medieval, but suggests that it was then strikingly painted—was designed by Gundulf, later bishop of Rochester, some time after 1070. Many shires were said to have groaned again under the imposition of further forced labour services in 1097, when a new wall was built around the Tower. Gundulf rebuilt Rochester Castle in stone for King William Rufus; but, in another instance of inefficient Norman planning, it was reconstructed a second time under Henry I.

The White Tower was described in the late 12th century not as a castle but as an *arx palatina*, a palatial stronghold. With its exquisite apsidal chapel, very similar to that in the even larger Colchester, it was more than a fortification, much as the rebuilt Castle Acre and the brand new Castle Rising were to be for their respective lords in the 1140s. Though palatial, however, they were all still castles. When it came to palaces, William the Conqueror did not stint himself either; but with royal palaces, unlike castles, there was a well-established English tradition (despite William of Malmesbury's contrast between the English living like sybarites in mean hovels, and Normans living with abstemious moderation in splendid Romanesque buildings). Edward the Confessor's *Life* mentions in passing a royal palace at Gloucester, which may reflect the initiation of Christmas crown-wearings in the

abbey church during his reign. William the Conqueror seems to
have adapted and extended Edward's palaces at Winchester and
Westminster. With palaces and halls, as with everything else, the
Normans did not believe in doing things by halves—literally so,
in the case of the new Westminster Hall, which King William
Rufus said was 'not half big enough' when he first saw it in 1094
(the labour services for its construction, in addition to the new
wall around the Tower and a bridge over the Thames, were still
eliciting groans from the *Anglo-Saxon Chronicle* in 1097). This
quotation may owe more to Henry of Huntingdon's familiarity
with Suetonius than to reality (though Herbert Losinga, bishop
of Norwich, had not been able to track down a copy in England in
the 1090s). But if Rufus did not say it, he should have done. His
alleged comment epitomizes the arrogant Norman determination
to build bigger than anyone: Westminster Hall was probably
the largest secular building in contemporary Europe. But not
necessarily better: it was yet another grandiose botched job.
The buttresses and arcading on the east and west sides are

17. Westminster Hall, built by William Rufus, and scene of the opulent
feasts described by Gaimar

misaligned by four feet which, like the shoddy stonework, betrays incompetence. Perhaps William Rufus failed to notice this error because he was dazzled by the interior paintwork, at least some of which was in blue and red; or perhaps size was all that mattered to him. That this could well have been the lay perspective is suggested by Gaimar, who recounts how the king presided there over opulent feasts, with three hundred gorgeously appareled ushers to conduct the guests up the steps. Perhaps their garb included the sort of fancy footwear which gratified the king's fetish, if William of Malmesbury is to be believed.

Crown-wearing in York, Christmas 1069

The architectural evidence for the Conquest corroborates the picture given by written sources. There was an elaborate pretence at continuity, but the forms in which continuity was embodied rapidly transformed the country into something quite new. The true extent of William the Conqueror's respect for England's heritage is revealed at the conclusion of the harrying of the North at Christmas 1069. He had successfully faced down the rebels' attempts, supported by a Danish invasion, to anoint Edgar *ætheling* as king in York. Edgar had, as we saw, been elected as king in 1066, in the aftermath of the defeat at Hastings; but that desperate last stand had soon come to nothing. The attempted reprise in 1069 had prompted the Conqueror to devastate the region so effectively that refugees straggled as far south as Evesham Abbey, where they 'lay about in the graveyard' and Abbot Æthelwig set up a field kitchen, thereby showing a twinge of Christian charity to a few of the many compatriot victims of the regime he served so assiduously.

In order to ram home his triumph, William ordered that his regalia should be shipped from the royal treasury in Winchester Castle to York. According to Orderic Vitalis, the king arranged that his Christmas ceremonial crown-wearing would take place not as usual in Gloucester Abbey, but in the Old English York Minster, where Edgar *ætheling* would probably have been anointed if the rebellion had succeeded. Yet, as the version of the *Anglo-Saxon Chronicle* written in the (very recently deceased) Archbishop Ealdred's household bitterly relates, the king's troops had recently 'ravaged the city, and made St Peter's Minster an object of scorn, and ravaged and humiliated all the others'. This disgraceful episode had, according to John of Worcester's *Chronicle*, occurred a mere eight days after Ealdred's death, his final illness allegedly brought on by distress at the arrival in the Humber estuary of a Danish invasion force, in league with Edgar *ætheling* and various English nobles. The Norman desecration of York Minster had been just as pointed an act as the king's determination to stage his Christmas crown-wearing in its ruins.

The behaviour of the royal forces in York in 1069 had therefore been even more sacrilegious than that in which they had indulged themselves during William's coronation in London on Christmas Day 1066. Then they had torched many other buildings but spared Westminster Abbey. In 1069 in York, they destroyed the cathedral, and other churches too. Orderic does not say so, not least because he was presumably drawing on the lost ending of William of Poitiers, but the image one should conjour to mind is of the Conqueror, resplendent in his royal insignia, with the assembled clergy singing *laudes* to him, enthroned in the burnt out shell of York Minster, with snow gently falling through the charred embers of the roof. It was, to the day, the third anniversary of his accession as king, with which the Conquest had been consummated. Close by was the fresh grave of the man who had consecrated him king.

Archbishop Thomas, Ealdred's Norman successor, found, according to the York historian Hugh the Chanter, 'the metropolitan church of St Peter burnt out, and its ornaments, charters, and privileges burnt and lost'. When he decided to rebuild the cathedral which the king's troops had destroyed, he did so on the site of the Roman military headquarters, the *principia*, exactly in the centre of Roman York, with the high altar probably close to the sacred *aedes*, or 'chapel of standards', and the centre of the apse on the centre of the Roman north–south street. The builders excavated the Roman foundations, and made careful use of them. It is impossible to tell whether Archbishop Thomas chose this site because Constantine had been proclaimed emperor there. What seems unlikely is that he chose it because it was the site of St Peter's. Extensive excavations in the late 1960s found no trace of the Old English cathedral under the present one. Indeed, it is not known where it was located in York. Like so much of Old England, it has disappeared without trace. This combination of brutal force, meticulous ceremonial propriety, and total eradication of the true (as opposed to fabricated) Old English past perfectly encapsulates the Norman Conquest of England.

Conclusion

Soon after 1120, Eadmer wrote in uncharacteristically forthright terms to the monks of Glastonbury, who were claiming that they possessed the relics of St Dunstan because their forebears had stolen his body from Canterbury. He professed astonishment that they should tout such a tall tale:

> especially because it is said that these tales were made up by Englishmen. Why did you not consult someone from overseas, where they have greater experience, more learning, and know better how to make up such stories? You could even have paid someone to make up a plausible lie for you on a matter of such importance.

Usually, of course, Eadmer expressed himself with a deft obliqueness, as in his satirical redrafting of Duke William's claim to the English throne. On this occasion, however, he could not keep his outrage under wraps, and revealed his true opinion of those overseas pens who could so easily be hired by the continental prelates who now presided over English churches, and by others. Perhaps he was thinking of William of Poitiers and his ilk. When Glastonbury Abbey subsequently made the mistake of commissioning a work from the renowned William of Malmesbury, rather than some foreign hack, he carefully avoided endorsing the claim. Accordingly, a long corrective passage had to be spliced into his *De antiquitate*

Glastonie ecclesie in order to remedy the—from a Glastonbury perspective—deficiency.

Eadmer's splenetic outburst and William of Malmesbury's high-minded wriggling reveal that both historians had a conception of where to draw the line between truth and falsehood. But they did so about details in the history of two monastic houses. It was because this detail touched the interests of his own house that Eadmer was so enraged. On a grander, national scale, however, they failed to find any convincing alternative to the story peddled in its extant form by William of Jumièges and William of Poitiers. There was no other way of explaining how the Conquest fitted on to earlier English history. From the very start, it seems, this story had underpinned the tenurial settlement in conquered England, and therefore Domesday Book's attempt to engross that settlement. It is what the monks of Malmesbury and Canterbury, and of the many other houses to which their histories (and others) were disseminated, would have listened to as they ate. These books were written, and punctuated, for reading aloud. Given that even Lanfranc, that uncompromising proponent of monastic regeneration, expected the model modern monk to read only one book a year, what little history they knew must for the most part have been absorbed aurally at mealtimes. Even this could happen only when the rule of St Benedict was applied flexibly, because the rule specified that the collation should be a scriptural or a patristic passage.

The victors' account of history was the only one to survive, just as the victors' buildings had everywhere replaced those of Edward the Confessor's England. The very language was soon to atrophy and virtually to disappear, at least in writing. By the late 11th century, it seems that only one manuscript of the *Anglo-Saxon Chronicle* was still being maintained, and that solitary survivor of the tradition of vernacular historical writing eventually fizzled out in 1154. According to Orderic, William the Conqueror had struggled to master Old English so that he could understand pleading in land disputes. If Orderic was not just being sardonic, it seems unlikely that the king would have bothered to try very hard. He had quislings like Wulfstan and Æthelwig, and, interestingly, in the early days, Waltheof. They were suitably rewarded for their collaboration, though Waltheof paid with his head for his collusion or participation in the rebellion of 1075, and was thereafter transformed into a symbol of English national sentiment. (Orderic, as a jobbing hack, was the first to write up his life for Crowland Abbey.) Surviving English prelates displayed no ambivalence with respect to their king. Like Æthelwig, Wulfstan remained steadfastly loyal. One of his rewards was to be allowed to conduct the Domesday Survey of the lands of his church, and to have the resulting self-assessment inserted into the Book. The church of Worcester was specially favoured with an exemption from the attentions of the Domesday commissioners.

It is, therefore, unlikely that William the Conqueror felt the need to bone up on Old English. However, the feat of the stenographers working on the Domesday Survey, interpreting English, French, and Latin testimony, and reducing it all to a standardized glossary of novel Norman Latin terms, was a formidable one. That they were almost certainly foreigners is revealed by the misunderstandings of English concepts and institutions embodied in the Book. The main scribe of the fair copy was an Englishman from Durham—one of William of St Calais' household—but the terminology he copied out so meticulously from earlier drafts (such as the *Liber Exoniensis*) had been devised by someone from overseas—perhaps by Bishop William himself. Whoever was responsible, the technical terminology, like the historical framework of the Survey, was, in terms of English tradition, a fictional, foreign import. Once the testimony of the English jurors had been translated into the new Latin jargon, the English language ceased to be of much moment, officially speaking. And because it was no longer a language of royal government, it soon became obsolete for many other purposes too. In the 12th century, the chronicler of Ramsey Abbey moaned about the 'difficulty and tedium' involved in translating all the abbey's Old English charters into Latin.

We do not know whether Lanfranc ever tried to mug up Old English. He told Pope Alexander that the language had been unknown to him when he was appointed as archbishop in 1070. He also claimed, perhaps sanctimoniously, perhaps facetiously, to be a 'new Englishman'. It seems unlikely that he tried any harder than the king to learn the language. He did not need to be fluent in Old English in order to exploit English testimony. Æthelric, the decrepit bishop of Selsey, was so infirm that he was literally wheeled out in a cart at the land plea held at Penenden Heath to testify concerning the long standing rights of the church of Canterbury. The true extent of Lanfranc's respect for the old man is revealed by the fact that he was at about this time orchestrating Æthelric's deposition. The procedure was in the pope's view so blatantly uncanonical that he was moved to write a letter of rebuke to the king. It took a lot to provoke Alexander II to reprimand William the Conqueror, or to thwart his old tutor. The esteem in which Lanfranc held the English is also suggested by William of Malmesbury's report that he denounced Bishop Wulfstan, the sole surviving English bishop, as illiterate. Many charges could be laid against Wulfstan, but illiteracy is not a plausible one. Wulfstan was a great believer in the importance of written records: he commissioned Hemming's cartulary, to preserve the records of Worcester's properties in a dangerously litigious age, and the Worcester *Chronicle* now attributed to John. Gosceclin of St Bertin, that great admirer of Norman architecture, nevertheless denounced the Normans for confusing illiteracy with wisdom and sanctity; so illiteracy was clearly a standard monastic insult. But Lanfranc's disparagement of the conquered English went deeper than the cynical exploitation of English testimony, or the trading of conventional monastic jibes.

His canon law collection, as we have seen, embodied his programme for the reform of the English church. Amongst legal

18. (a) Cambridge, Trinity College MS. B. 16. 44, p. 328. This is Lanfranc's personal copy of his canon law collection. The marginal 'A' (for 'attende') may be in his own hand; similar marks throughout the manuscript draw attention to references which were of particular interest to him. This one, beside canon 75 of the Fourth Council of Toledo, is concerned with the topical issue of the anathematization of usurpers

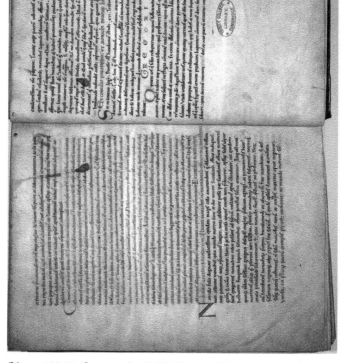

(b) pp. 406–07: the second and third letters of Pope Clement III to Lanfranc copied here are in the hand of Eadmer, sometime Canterbury scribe, amanuensis to Archbishop Anselm, and historian

sources bearing on the Conquest, it is second in importance only to Domesday Book, in the framework of which it provided, as we have seen, a vital element; but it has been largely neglected by historians. It was a version of a 9th-century Frankish compilation, known of the Pseudo-Isidorian decretals, which became the basis for all canon law collections until the mid-12th century. As such, and unsurprisingly in view of the compilation's title, which sought to locate it in 7th-century Spain, it includes the proceedings of all the councils of Toledo held in the 6th and 7th centuries under the auspices of the Visigothic conquerors of Roman Spain. These were of unquestionable authority, because they were sanctioned by inclusion in the collection, ostensibly promulgated under papal authority. They were deemed to have the status of church councils. It was Visigothic Spain, not—as Lanfranc speciously argued—Old England, which provided the template for Canterbury's primacy over all British churches. Canterbury aped Toledo's primacy over the churches of Spain, as defined in the Toledan councils. Toledo's unique role in the consecration of Visigothic kings would have been especially pertinent, in view of the (unrealized) threat to consecrate Edgar *ætheling* king in York in 1069.

Visigothic Spain proved to be such a rich source of precedents for Lanfranc precisely because it was a conquered country. The Visigothic councils therefore dealt with all manner of problems— such as the legal relations between conquerors and conquered— which were relevant to the Normans in England. No wonder Lanfranc, in a fly leaf to his own annotated copy, invoked an anathema on the head of anyone who removed it from the library of Christ Church, Canterbury. He envisaged constant reference being made to it. It provided a programme for ecclesiastical reform, but also—in so far as it was possible to distinguish between the two—a programme for an elite regime of conquerors ruling a large, surly, subject population, with quite different (and arguably more civilized) traditions, and distinct codes of law. In other words, it was a handbook for regime change, 11th-century style. No wonder every major church had to have a copy. For all their brutality, the Normans had from the Conquest's inception sought to implement it by the book.

When William de Longchamp (d. 1197), chancellor of King Richard I (1189–99), felt a call of nature, he was apt to say 'Let's go and do an English.' By his day, of course, much had changed; in particular, the legal distinctions between French and English evident in, for instance, the *murdrum* fine, had all but disappeared. Yet the crude snobbery he voiced towards the English was not a development of the intervening century and a half. It was there from the start, as William of Poitiers' passing slurs on English national character reveal. The difference between them was that William de Longchamp did not restrict himself to snide asides. There was no longer any need to maintain the pretence of continuity. It had achieved its objective during the Conqueror's reign. He could be quite uninhibited about denigrating the English in the coarsest of terms.

Old England had been obliterated long ago; in so far as any vestiges of it remained, they did so mainly in the histories of Eadmer, William of Malmesbury, and Henry of Huntingdon, and lesser writers of the same period, such as John of Worcester. Their attempts to reconstruct Old England have determined the way it is studied and understood ever since. They still do so. There is no alternative. That is telling testimony to the success of the Norman conquerors in eradicating the real Old England, and fabricating one in their own image. The early 12th-century historians of England had only very limited success in penetrating behind that fabrication. In conquering the kingdom of England, the Normans had conquered its past as well as its future. Or as Eadmer might have put it, the 'plausible lie' had prevailed, and the English had in truth been treated much as the haughty William de Longchamp felt free to imply.

References and further reading

Sources

The best translation of the various manuscripts of the *Anglo-Saxon Chronicle* is: *The Anglo-Saxon Chronicle: A Revised Translation*, ed. D. Whitelock, with D. C. Douglas and S. I. Tucker (London, 1961).

The works of most of the Latin chronicles are now available in superb parallel text editions:

Vita Ædwardi Regis, ed. F. Barlow, 2nd edn. (Oxford, 1992)

William of Jumièges, *Gesta Normannorum Ducum*, ed. E. M. C. van Houts, 2 vols (Oxford, 1992–5)

William of Poitiers, *Gesta Guillelmi*, ed. M. M. Chibnall (Oxford, 1998)

Orderic Vitalis, *The Ecclesiastical History*, ed. M. M. Chibnall, 6 vols (Oxford, 1969–80)

William of Malmesbury, *Gesta Regum Anglorum*, ed. R. A. B. Mynors, R. M. Thomson, and M. Winterbottom, 2 vols (Oxford, 1998–9)

William of Malmesbury, *Gesta Pontificum Anglorum*, ed. M. Winterbottom and R. M. Thomson, 2 vols (Oxford, 2007)

William of Malmesbury, *Saints' Lives*, ed. M. Winterbottom and R. M. Thomson (Oxford, 2002)

Henry of Huntingdon, *Historia Anglorum*, ed. D. Greenway (Oxford, 1996)

Eadmer of Canterbury, *Lives and Miracles of Saints Oda, Dunstan, and Oswald*, ed. B. J. Muir and A. J. Turner (Oxford, 2006)

John of Worcester, *Chronicle*, ed. R. R. Darlington and P. McGurk, 3 vols (Oxford, 1995–)

Thomas of Marlborough, *History of the Abbey of Evesham*, ed. J. Sayers and L. Watkiss (Oxford, 2003)

Historia Ecclessie Abbendonensis, ed. J. G. H. Hudson, 2 vols (Oxford, 2002–7)

Eadmer of Canterbury, *Lives and Miracles of Saints Oda, Dunstan, and Oswald*, ed. B. J. Muir and A. J. Turner (Oxford, 2006).

Also:

Eadmer, *History of Recent Events*, tr. G. Bosanquet (London, 1964)

For translations of both volumes of Domesday Book, see the Penguin edition:

Domesday Book, ed. G. Martin and A. Williams (Harmondsworth, 2002).

The Letters of Lanfranc, Archbishop of Canterbury, ed. H. Clover and M. Gibson (Oxford, 1979), are written in deadpan bureaucratese, and need to be read with suspicion.

The Bayeux Tapestry, ed. D. M. Wilson (London, 1985), is the most sumptuously illustrated edition; now reproduced in *The Bayeux Tapestry: Digital Edition*, ed. M. K. Foys (Scholarly Digital Editions, 2003).

Literature

The most detailed account, which still repays careful reading, is E. A. Freeman, *The Norman Conquest of England*, 6 vols (Oxford, 1869–79).

For a very different view to that taken here, see R. Bartlett, *England under the Norman and Angevin Kings: 1075-1225* (Oxford, 2000); for the view taken here amplified and extended, see G. Garnett, *Conquered England: Kingship, Succession, and Tenure: 1066-1166* (Oxford, 2007). More straightforward accounts are M. M. Chibnall, *Anglo-Norman England* (Oxford, 1986) and B. Golding, *Conquest and Colonisation: The Normans in Britain, 1066-1100*, 2nd edn. (London, 2001).

Many of the most thought-provoking recent essays are collected in J. C. Holt, *Colonial England, 1066-1215* (London, 1997).

On William the Conqueror, see D. Bates, *William the Conqueror* (London, 1989); for most of the *dramatis personae*, see H. C. G. Matthew and B. Harrison (eds.), *The Oxford Dictionary of National Biography* (Oxford, 2004).

On Domesday Book, see, in addition to Holt's essays, V. H. Galbraith, *The Making of Domesday Book* (Oxford, 1960); R. Fleming, *Kings and Lords in Conquest England* (Cambridge, 1991); R. W. Finn,

The Domesday Inquest and the Making of Domesday Book (London, 1961); J. C. Holt (ed.), *Domesday Studies* (Woodbridge, 1987). F. W. Maitland, *Domesday Book and Beyond* (Cambridge, 1897) uses Domesday to burrow into the Old English past, and is still the most impressive book on the period.

On law, see also F. Pollock and F. W. Maitland, *The History of English Law*, 2 vols, 2nd edn. (Cambridge, 1898); J. G. H. Hudson, *Land, Law, and Lordship in Anglo-Norman England* (Oxford, 1994); J. G. H. Hudson, *The Formation of the English Common Law: Law and Society in England from the Conquest to Magna Carta* (Harlow, 1996).

On military matters, see M. K. Lawson, *The Battle of Hastings 1066* (Stroud, 2002), and the essays collected in M. Strickland (ed.), *Anglo-Norman Warfare* (Woodbridge, 1992); reading H. Spelman, 'The Original, Growth, Propagation and Condition of Feuds and Tenures by Knight-Service in England', *Reliquiae Spelmaniannae* (Oxford, 1698), which was written in 1639, is an illuminating and chastening experience.

On Romanesque architecture, see R. Gem, *Studies in English Pre-Romanesque and Romanesque Architecture*, 2 vols (London, 2003); E. Fernie, *The Architecture of Norman England* (Oxford, 2000); on manuscripts, see R. Gameson, *Manuscripts of Early Norman England (c. 1066–1130)* (Oxford, 1999); on these and other aspects of Romanesque art, G. Zarnecki, J. Holt, and T. Holland (eds.), *English Romanesque Art: 1066–1200* (London, 1984).

A. Williams, *The English and the Norman Conquest* (Woodbridge, 1995) gives an insight into the predicament of the conquered.

For more detail on these and other themes, see the extensive bibliography for the Norman Conquest of England Special Subject, available via the website of the Modern History Faculty, Oxford University: http://www.history.ox.ac.uk/.

Chronology

	25 September. King Harold victorious at the battle of Stamford Bridge
	28–29 September. Norman invasion fleet arrives at Pevensey
	14 October. Battle of Hastings
	25 December. William the Conqueror crowned in Westminster Abbey
1067	William returns in triumph to Normandy, with many important English captives in his train
1068	Prior to 23 March. Rebellion in the West Country, submission of Exeter
	11 May, Whitsun. Coronation of Matilda as queen in Westminster Abbey
1069	11 September. Death of Archbishop Ealdred
	Rebellion and harrying of the North
	Christmas. Crown-wearing in ruins of York Minster
1070	7 or 11 April. Coronation by papal legates at Winchester; deposition of English prelates commences
	15 August. Lanfranc appointed archbishop of Canterbury
	Battle Abbey founded
1072	c. 8 April. Council at Winchester, reconvened at Windsor on 27 May (Whitsun)
	See of Dorchester moved to Lincoln
1075	Rebellion led by Roger, earl of Hereford, Ralph Guader, and arguably Waltheof, earl of Northumbria
	Prior to 28 August. Council at London
	See of Sherborne moved to Old Sarum; see of Selsey moved to Chichester
1076	1 April. Council at Winchester
	31 May. Earl Waltheof executed for complicity in rebellion
1078	Æthelwig, abbot of Evesham, dies
1079	Construction of Winchester Cathedral begins
1080	Construction of York Minster begins

1085	Christmas. Domesday Survey planned at gathering for festival crown-wearing at Gloucester
1086	1 August. 'Oath of Salisbury' and presentation to king of 'writings' produced by the Survey
1087	9 September. Death of William the Conqueror at Rouen
	26 September. Coronation of William Rufus in Westminster Abbey
1089	Construction of Gloucester Abbey begins
1092	Old Sarum Cathedral consecrated
1093	15 July. Winchester Cathedral consecrated
	29 July. Construction of Durham Cathedral begins
1094	Wulfstan, bishop of Worcester, dies
1096	Sometime see of Elmham, currently in Thetford, moved to Norwich
1100	2 August. William Rufus killed in a hunting accident; buried in Winchester Cathedral
	5 August. Henry I crowned in Westminster Abbey

Table 1: The English Royal House (simplified)

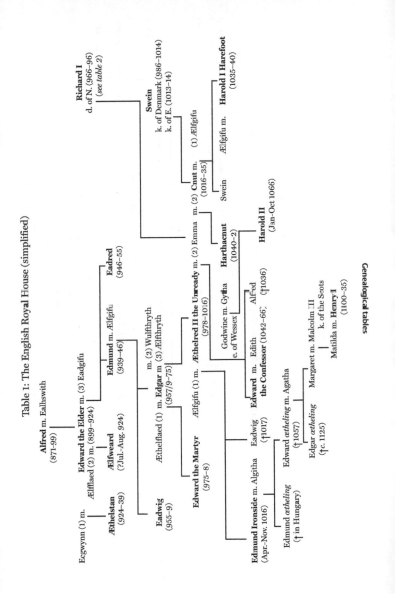

The Norman Conquest

Table 2: The Norman Ducal House (Simplified)

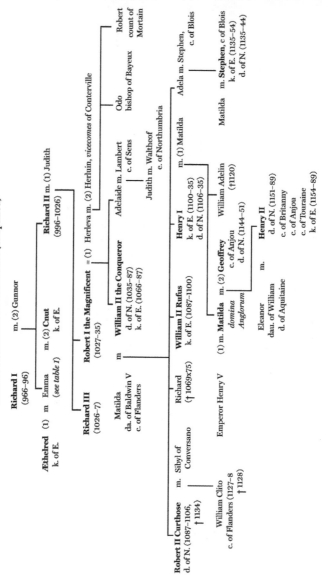

140

Index

Expand your collection of
VERY SHORT INTRODUCTIONS